LASTING MEMORIES

LASTING MEMORIES

A Complete Guide to Creating a Family Scrapbook

ANITA L. HICKINBOTHAM

Contemporary Books

Chicago New York San Francisco Lisbon London Madrid Mexico City
Milan New Delhi San Juan Seoul Singapore Sydney Toronto

Contents

Preface

*L*ifting the cover of a scrapbook is the beginning of an adventure. If you're looking at an old family album, the images you find in it may be vaguely familiar faces that are gauzy reflections of your brothers, sisters, cousins, and even your own mirrored image. You might be looking at a scrapbook you made during your high school years, or maybe you're ready to start a new scrapbook, with a recent batch of photographs, memorabilia, and stories.

Each piece in an album tells a little bit of someone's life story—a colorful image of their perspective and personality and of the activities they enjoyed. With each album, you'll learn more about your family *and* yourself. Perhaps you will even discover previously unseen threads, the commonalities that link you together and that connect you with your ancestors in new ways.

Scrapbooks: A Link to the Past, a Gift to the Future

"Would you like to have these?" my mother asked, handing me a large cardboard box she had just hauled in from the car.

Curious, I set the bulky parcel on my dining room table and lifted the overlapping creased flaps to discover the box's contents. Neatly stacked inside were six books, similar in size, with yellowing bits of newspaper protruding from the worn edges.

"They were your grandmother's scrapbooks," Mom explained. "I haven't looked at them since before she died."

I hadn't known these remnants of Grandma's life existed, but for several months I had been sifting through old family photographs and fragments of written information, beginning to piece together some of my family's history.

Grandma had been gone nine years now; Grandpa, twelve. What would these volumes reveal? What mementos pasted here would give me a glimpse into lives now silent? What stories would be told or secrets disclosed?

x ....

PREFACE

Old scrapbooks can fill in the details of our ancestors' lives and can give us ideas on what we could include in our own albums.

Already grateful for my mother's generous offer, I knew these treasures would unveil some new perspectives of the past; events of days gone by were about to be resurrected. I carefully lifted the first album from the box, thrilled by this good fortune.

The cover of the first volume was black, a lavish scrolled design embellishing it. Gold ink imprinted the center, with gently curved letters spelling "Scrap Book." A soiled golden cord still held most of the pages in place. I opened the book.

A cockeyed price tag was still firmly stuck to the album's inside cover. It read "S. S. Kresge Co., 39 cents, 3-12-49." I remembered that store, long since closed, and pictured my grandmother, then only forty, walking in to purchase the book I now held. Kresge's had stood prominently at the corner of Main and North Park Streets on Mansfield's square. Pasted beside the tiny tag was a May 1949 cover of *Household* magazine showing a beautiful mother nestling her new baby in one arm and a generous bouquet of red roses in the other. Still adhered to the corner of the picture was the subscription mailing label with Grandma's name and 1949 address. "What had drawn her to this particular picture?" I wondered.

The albums were put together in a haphazard fashion. Some had no obvious progression. Perhaps she had taken a box of mementos gathered through the years, jumbled from occasional rereading, and stuck the mementos to the pages in the order they happened to surface. Maybe she began in chronological order, frugally using the remaining spaces wherever a clipping fit. Either way, it was a window into her quirky personality.

With delight I viewed the combination of items Grandma had assembled. She'd pasted thank-you notes for baby gifts that she'd sent beside obituaries of relatives, acquaintances, or prominent community figures. *TV Guide* covers depicting favorite shows or glamorous actors were glued next to results of bowling contests. A faded newspaper clipping, tucked deep inside a tattered envelope, whispered details of a long-ago family divorce. They were small tokens of life and death, of victories and struggles, of social celebrations and public embarrassments. Some questions were answered; now new questions formed.

Nonetheless, the contents of these fragile albums were painting a picture of Grandma. Each souvenir added a brushstroke of color to her portrait, and I was getting a glimpse of this petite woman's varying hues. The scraps she chose to cut and paste revealed not only her interests and hobbies, but her beliefs and values as well. In my mind, her role as my grandmother was giving way to my discovery of her as a woman.

Scrapbooks are powerful vessels that travel across time, connecting one generation to the next. Just as my grandmother's albums brought parts of her life to me, the ones you fashion will likewise impact those who linger over their pages in the years ahead.

As you read and use this book, it is my hope that you will be inspired by the real-life experiences of others who have made scrapbooks, encouraged to create by the artwork, helped by the tips, and spurred to preserve the stories only you can tell.

Caution: working on a scrapbook may change your life! In these days of busy schedules and the frantic attempt to fit everything in, running a "rat race" tends to be the norm. You may find scrapbooking can adjust your perspective when taking the time to reflect on the past, savor the present, and consider the future, for then you are reminded of what is most important in life. My guess is that these quiet moments will produce more than a finished album. I wish you peace and enjoyment in the process!

Warmly,

Anita L. Hickinbotham

Acknowledgments

I am deeply grateful to the many people who joined me at various places on the road and during the journey of writing this book.

Thanks to the ones who came before me, for saving family correspondence, keeping diaries, and labeling family photographs, and especially to my grandmother, Hazel Altman, for making the scrapbooks that have been a significant connection to my heritage and an inspiration for my work.

Thanks to Monica Granitto, for giving me a copy of *Drawing on the Right Side of the Brain*, which proved to me that artistry could be learned, and for introducing me to archival scrapbooking products.

Thanks to Jeni Lewis, for encouraging me to put pen to paper and chart the course. Your input helped me consider the options and spurred me to take the first steps that eventually led to this version of the book.

Thanks to Jeanie Ruark, for your generosity in beautifully formatting the text and visuals for the first version of the manuscript. It undoubtedly helped to get it to the next step.

Thanks to my "signposts": my mother, Betty Myers, Helen Fritz, and Martin Myers, who believed this book was worth publishing and pointed me to Contemporary Books. Thank you for your confidence in this project.

Thanks to my editor, Anne Knudsen, for giving me the opportunity to get my ideas in print.

Thanks to the "fellow travelers" who joined me by allowing me to include their marvelous pictures and album pages: Anne Baker, Deb Deschner, Beth Feia, Aimee Ferguson, Steve and Brenda Fortney, Monica Granitto, Suzy Linger, Deb McKee, and Ellen Smith. I am especially grateful to Liz Bowie and Janet Keeler for entrusting me with their priceless family heirloom albums.

Thanks to the many archival researchers and technical specialists around the country who generously shared information, especially Anne Wilbur, Dan Burge, and Don Pierce.

For their patience and encouragement, I am grateful to Jan Zody, Deb Deschner, Mary Lou Haycook, and Thelma Stockwell.

For continuing love and prayers, which buoyed me more than I will probably ever know, I thank Peggy Brown, Cindy Falls, Saunnie Cassell, Cherrie Kent, Eunice Nethery, and the entire Nethery home group.

I am grateful to my wonderful sisters and brothers-in-law, Marcia Myers and Larry Williams and Laurie and Tom Beech, for their continual interest and unwavering support.

I owe special thanks to the following people who have impacted my life in significant ways that benefited me during this project: JoAnn Brucato Barlow, for prodding a class of sixth graders to put their thoughts, observations, and conclusions on paper; to my longtime friend Scott Gandert, who shares my love of writing; to Alan Roxburgh, whose words inspired me to let this book be drawn forth; and to Aimee Ferguson, who loves scrapbooking as much as I do.

I am also thankful for the memories I have of my father, Don Myers, who supported his daughters in pursuing their interests, and of Tim Barber, my pastor and friend, for showing me that the lane was lavender, teaching me about color specifically and life in general. I miss you both.

My extreme gratitude and thanks go to Beth S. E. Feia. You are a rare gem! Thank you for your willingness to be a sounding board, for your generous availability throughout the entire writing process, and for taking my little ones swimming and to Burton Park and Malabar Farm during the final stages of my writing. You have gone way beyond the call of duty and shown me true friendship!

I am grateful to the following people for their help with the Thomas Jefferson scrapbooks: Professor Robert M. S. McDonald and Christine Coalwell for sharing their thoughts and research files; Heather Moore at the University of Virginia, Alderman Library, Special Collections; Whitney Espich, Communications Officer at Monticello; Kerry Taylor, Monticello Registrar; and Gaye Wilson, librarian at the Monticello Research Department, for her help in arranging details for our visit to Monticello and seeing that we had everything we needed.

I am deeply indebted to the following companies for granting permission to include their products in this book: 3L Corp.; Accu-Cut® Systems; All Night Media, Inc.; The C-Thru Ruler Company; Canson, Inc.; Crafty Cutter; Creative Imaginations and Jone Hallmark (Bryce and Madeline Stickers); Creative Memories; Cut-It-Up; Dana Ward/Cheshire Recordings; Delta Technical Coatings; EK Success Ltd.; Ellison Craft and Design; Extra Special Products Corp.; Family Treasures, Inc.; Fiskars, Inc.; Frances Meyer, Inc.; Mary Engelbreit Studios; The Gifted Line/Michel & Co.; Mrs. Grossman's Paper Company; The Paper Patch; Pebbles, Inc.; Personal Stamp Exchange; R.A. Lang Card Co.; and Sakura of America.

Why Make Scrapbooks?

1

*W*onderfully descriptive family photographs are easy to find. They let us in on celebrations, warm our hearts with scenes of tender moments, or inspire us with a glimpse of a hardship faced that has been captured on film and transferred to paper. But what happens if details about the photographed moment are never recorded?

Without the identifying information, the value of these snapshots to a family can be lost after just one generation. You can try to guess when and where the photographs were taken and what the activity of the day was, but you'll have little clue as to the peripheral parts of the story. As time passes, no one remembers the names that identify the faces. You may be the owner of many unlabeled photos, if not entire boxes or photo albums full.

I purchased the photographs shown opposite on the same day in a small antique shop in Kensington, Maryland. I chose only a handful from thousands in that one room. Consider the number of orphaned photos in existence around the world!

These pictures are marvelous. They surely have colorful stories that could have accompanied them, yet few have any notation on the back. It is reasonable to assume that the pictures capturing group activities very likely have people in them with living descendants.

Scrapbooking offers you an opportunity to preserve your photos, stories, and memorabilia by placing them in albums, with the names and dates marked and details of the stories told, for your own pleasure and for the benefit and fun of your descendants.

What Is a Scrapbook?

Human beings have always strived to record thoughts in a lasting form. The development of alphabets enabled people to move from symbolic notation to readable words. With the introduction of Johannes Gutenberg's movable-type press in the mid-1400s, printed work began to flourish.

The first regularly published newspapers were issued in Germany in the 1600s, and growing availability enabled readers to easily dispose of these short-term-interest items. Yet readers had the opportunity to clip articles they wanted to save from the newspapers, the "scraps" that became the foundation of many scrapbooks. Readers could secure items on various topics in a volume to prevent them from getting lost and then use the compilation as a reference, a self-composed resource manual addressing anything they chose. Of course, saving memorabilia has always been popular, and in the last 150 years, photographs have been added to the list of items we desire to preserve.

Scrapbooks are marvelously effective time capsules because they can be a collection of these most dear possessions. They are photograph albums capturing activities and expressions that will never again occur in exactly the same way, journals giving rich descriptions of things observed and felt, and treasure chests of memorabilia carefully tucked away to be brought out and enjoyed on another day. They are miniature tapestries, weaving together the varying threads of happy and possibly not-so-happy times, and empty canvases waiting for an artist to portray each incident in whatever style he or she chooses, carefully defining each mood and activity. More than a showcase of highlights, hopefully our albums will record simple daily activities as well. They are real-life storybooks. And making them is a fun and rewarding experience!

Scrapbooking has come a long way. Victorian albums were often filled with cut-out papers that were lovely in design, rich in color, and reminiscent of lacy valentines. Voluptuous women, floral motifs, children, and birds were common subjects. Usually absent were captions or other notations that would indicate the tokens had sentimental value. Many ladies apparently salvaged these pretty pieces simply because they appreciated the detailed beauty and wanted to enjoy them again.

Scrapbooks have also been used as a personal notebook. Like my grandmother, many people used them to save their newspaper clippings and any other information of particular interest. But in these, artistic expression was usually minimal.

As cameras increased in popularity and availability, scrapbooking lost the attention of many. Families tended to have numerous photo albums but little written record of their lives.

Thankfully, the interest in making scrapbooks has been renewed, and men, women, and children are now creating albums that are lively and colorful. The introduction of photo-safe materials to the general public has heightened our awareness of preservation issues and helped us choose better-quality supplies. Where once materials and approach were limited, available supplies now let creativity abound—and scrapbookers are happily making use of the options.

Scrapbooks serve various purposes. They record your memories and help document history by the noting of names and dates. They give definition of who you are and mark your progress. While reminiscing over past events, you can appreciate those with whom you've shared them. They can draw your family together by the opportunity they offer you to consider the people you're highlighting and reflect on their personalities, interests, and uniqueness. Scrapbooks say "I love you" in a beautifully creative way. They can help you grieve a recently lost loved one by memorializing his or her special life in an album. Or a scrapbook can be a simple tool to teach a child the alphabet using the photos of people and places he or she knows and loves.

Some old scrapbooks were made only with clippings. The addition of photos and journaling tells a more complete story.

Developing Your Style

Scrapbooks have great potential as records of our lives, but making one doesn't have to be complicated. Actually it's a lot like first grade—paper, scissors, glue, and the delight of playfully going wherever your whims take you. Rare (or perhaps nonexistent) are scrapbookers who plan their entire page in detail before they start. More often, they will get a basic idea and develop it as they go.

Whether or not you consider yourself artistic, I encourage you to begin. I've heard some people say they're hesitant to start an album because future pages will make their first ones look bad. Nonsense! Would we refuse to learn to cook, practice sports, or play musical instruments simply because we couldn't begin at an advanced level? What would we tell our children if they said such things? And a scrapbook doesn't even have to be assembled in a highly decorative style. The most crucial objective is to get the photos and stories safely preserved for your family. The manner in which you do this can and should be of your choosing.

As your scrapbooking experience increases, you will undoubtedly find ways you prefer to approach the designing of your pages, and a style will evolve. Jan, a friendly grandmother who has been a longtime regular in my morning workshops, finds great delight in observing this development. Her eyes sparkle as she comments on the individuality coming forth. I share her view. Just as your life matures with the years, so your albums will likely evolve as you practice your skills and develop ideas.

Goals

It is helpful to have some goals in mind before you start, so take a few moments to consider what you'd like to accomplish. Remember, your scrapbook can be anything you want it to be. Many people make family albums, but others choose a particular theme: vacation, wedding, baby, a special holiday, or family pet. Some approach it from another angle, recording an interest or hobby, such as gardening or the building of a new home. Fortunate are the recipients of a scrapbook given as a gift commemorating a graduation, milestone birthday, anniversary, or retirement.

Think about which stories you want to begin preserving, the album's subject, what photos and memorabilia you have on hand to include, and where you might set up an out-of-the-way worktable.

It is important to secure your photographs in a photo-safe album. Many photo albums and some scrapbooks on the market can actually contribute to the deterioration of your treasured pictures. Familiarize yourself with the industry's terminology. You will want to know what *acid, lignin,* and *PVC* are and how they affect your photos. Understanding the lingo will help you choose products wisely and will keep you from shortening the life of your photographs (see Appendix).

Another aspect of the photo-safety issue is what to do with your memorabilia. You may have saved programs, ticket stubs, and noteworthy newspaper clippings. With a little preparation you can have the freedom of including these time-capturing mementos in your albums without damaging the photographs (see chapter 4).

As you begin working, you will want to keep in mind that the photos should generally be the focal point of the page (the place your eye is drawn to most quickly). There are a million decorative options available, and they are best used to enhance the pictures and story rather than compete with or overpower them.

Build your page carefully to achieve a good balance.

Work in a manner you enjoy. If quick and easy is your style—great! Perhaps you love detail and have the artistic skill to create beautifully intricate pages. Then go for it! Forcing yourself to work in someone else's style will probably cause you to abandon the whole project. So, trust your instincts, convey your unique ideas in the telling of your stories, have fun, and let your pages be a personal expression from your heart and hand.

How This Book Can Help You

This book is intended to help you in several ways. It addresses the key parts of a scrapbook: images, memorabilia, and words. It gives guidelines for composition and the use of color. It covers the foundational materials and tools and provides examples of hundreds of ways to use them. It suggests ideas to stimulate your memory in order to more accurately record past events and fully depict recent ones. It gives you some information on how to find high-quality products. It offers many tips to make the scrapbooking venture efficient and fun. It also includes true stories showing you what scrapbooks can be and their potential effect on those who read them.

You will notice that although there are completed scrapbook pages shown in this book as examples, my greater goal is to offer you pieces that may be combined in a multitude of ways to help you create one-of-a-kind pages. I hope to show you how to "translate" ideas and help you to think creatively, giving you more options than any single book could hold. I hope that by teaching you how to fish rather than giving you a fish, you'll be fed for a lifetime with the enjoyment and development of a newfound creativity and the motivation to tell your stories.

You can include many kinds of memorabilia in your album.

2

Getting Started

*S*o, you've decided to start a scrapbook. Where is the best place to begin? Working through the steps in this chapter will help clarify your direction and help you achieve the end result you desire. A bit of time spent on these will have you ready to start your first page.

Choosing the Theme of Your Album

The very first step is deciding the theme of the album you want to make. Your goal may be to start with your ancestors, placing the family photos in chronological order. Maybe you will decide to compile an album of your immediate family's story. Or perhaps there is a new baby in the house, and you want to capture every detail of growth and developing personality. (For more ideas see Appendix.) The theme you choose and the quantity of material you include will determine the album size you will need.

Create your album from whatever angle interests you the most. Your unique perspective and the style with which you record it will help you create this collection of memories. I have seen some splendid albums made by people who have taken an unusual approach. They exemplify the creativity that abounds when we let our special interests come forth.

jacie

January 1995

A great example of this came from a woman named Fran, who wanted my input regarding an album she was putting together. Fran had a prized collection of photographs of the brides in her family that spanned more than a hundred years. She was making an album that would contain only these elegant pictures, the names of each couple, and the dates of their weddings. Whatever your interest and motivation, consider a few specifics about the direction you will go. The workshop at the end of this chapter will help you with this.

What to Include in Your Scrapbook

Of course you are interested in including family events and celebrations in your scrapbooks. Birthdays, anniversaries, and holiday festivities with the traditions built into them are important links that connect the generations. These special times that you share create some of your most vivid memories.

But there are other aspects of life that are worth including in your albums as well. The record of occupations and hobbies makes a wonderful entry in the record of a family's history. They are the things that fill a typical day and are expressions of your interests and creativity.

For many, spiritual roots, traditions, and practices are at the core of life. They may significantly shape and impact you even in your daily routines. If these foundational beliefs and values are of the utmost importance to you, you certainly want to pass them on.

"Only be careful, and watch yourselves closely so that you do not forget the things your eyes have seen or let them slip from your heart as long as you live. Teach them to your children and to their children after them" (Deut. 4:9). For me, scrapbooking provides the opportunity to record for my family God's faithfulness to us, the insights we have gleaned, the hardships we have overcome, and the prayers that have been answered.

One thing I have noticed from seeing hundreds of scrapbooks is how rarely I come across one that has recorded a person's own journey. It is easy to snap photos of your adorable children and write their stories or to compile albums about your ancestors, but it appears that not many have taken the time to record specific events that have influenced and shaped their own lives.

Take a moment to reflect on what has made you who you are—the things you dreamed you'd do in life (and the ones you're still dreaming of), the lessons learned from struggles, and the obstacles you've surmounted. Please consider

including some of these. They have brought richness to your life and will add depth to your album.

Let your sense of humor be expressed through your scrapbook. Some of the most delightful albums I've seen are threaded with bits of whimsy that add to the visual fun of the page and also warm the reader's heart. The element of surprise draws the reader through the scrapbook, with anticipation of what he or she will discover on the next page and how that event will be described.

MY APPROACH TO SCRAPBOOKING

There are a wide variety of perspectives regarding how scrapbooks should be compiled, what you should or shouldn't include, how decorative they should be, and what products are safe to use. I will share my views with you here.

My love of scrapbooks has developed from the time I've spent enjoying the album my mother made for me as I was growing up. Mom carefully glued into my scrapbook party favors, napkins, and invitations; newspaper articles; and awards. I love having these pieces of my past. When my husband, John, and I became engaged, I purchased a large scrapbook to begin keeping a record of our life together. As the children came along, I bought each of them an album and immediately began enclosing photos and memorabilia. Discovering my grandmother through her scrapbooks fueled my interest even more, as the albums revealed the value of passing our stories down through the generations.

I think combining photos, journaling, and memorabilia in a scrapbook is the most captivating way of telling our stories. Unfortunately, I assembled my early books using construction paper for color and rubber cement for mounting. In spite of some damage, they are in relatively good shape and certainly cherished mementos. I encourage including memorabilia but doing so in a way that will help protect these pieces and the photographs they are placed near.

I view my scrapbook as a permanent compilation I am leaving behind, which I believe will tell the stories of my family most successfully because of the variety of things included. My goal is to do this as thoroughly as I can, being careful in regard to photo safety.

The scrapbooking industry has boomed, resulting in a huge influx of products on the market. I try to find the photo-safety information about products I am interested in using, then decide whether to include them in my album. There are some great companies serving scrapbookers. They are proud of the levels of quality they have achieved and gladly share information with interested customers. Look for companies that research well and help their customers by making archival information available (also see the Source Guide).

I want to make use of the creative options on the market. At the same time, I want to be careful not to choose products that are likely to damage my photos. The Photographic Activity Test (P.A.T.) determines if a product can be used near photographs without damaging them. Note that some of the products shown in this book have not yet been P.A.T. tested but are included because they fit the basic archival requirements for their type of product (acid-free, lignin-free, pigment ink, and so forth), because I like their design, and to serve as a decorative example for those types of products. More and more companies are having their products tested to be sure they are photo-safe. Check for updated information. If there is a product line you want to use in your album but it hasn't been P.A.T. approved, call and encourage the manufacturer to take that step. The scrapbooking community can help move the market in a good direction.

Use photo corners or safe plastic sleeves to secure old family photos in your scrap-books, since others in the family may like to make copies of them. Or, instead of putting the original photos in your album you might like to make copies of them. You probably have an abundance of photos from more recent days, and hopefully have kept the nega-tives. If you have, then the pictures are easily reproduced, and you can secure the originals in your album with permanent adhesives that will keep the compilation of images intact.

Some scrapbookers like to keep their pages simple, with the goal of getting the job done and staying current—a very good goal! Others love the artistry and creative options, and they enjoy spending time on the decorative elements of the page. Either way is acceptable and has benefits. Those of the former persuasion may indeed get more of the story told, while those of the latter will leave a fingerprint of their creativity behind that may enhance the memories and recorded stories for their families.

I love a colorful, playful display for my children's albums and a more classic look for the ancestral albums. And when working with older photographs, I try to have the style of the era reflected on the page. I think it captures the time frame all the more.

You may certainly make your album in any manner you choose, but I suggest that you consider having your duplicate photos (and/or negatives) safely filed—possibly at a relative's home. It is especially good to save them if you are going to cut the photographs you are using in your scrapbook. It will give you "memory insurance" for the future.

Organizing Your Photographs

The fastest way to begin an album is to use photographs and memorabilia from a recent event. With those in hand, it will be easy to get started on making your first album pages. If, however, you are making a heritage album or developing a theme that spans many years, you first need to organize your materials so that important items aren't accidentally omitted or overlooked. Be sure to look through photo albums, boxes of loose photos, and in places where you may have tucked away memorabilia related to the themes.

Once all the materials are gathered, begin a general sorting by person, topic, decade, or year. Label any unmarked photos with as much information as you know using a photo-marking pen. Be sure to label new photos as soon as possible for accuracy of dates and names. This prevents you, or someone else, from having to do the guesswork later.

If you are working with pictures spanning several generations, file them first by decade only. (For lesser quantities, filing by the year will probably be manageable.) As you are ready to work on a section, pull the file and continue sorting by year, then by season, month, and day. This approach requires several sortings, but it allows you to narrow down as needed and get started more quickly without worrying about having missed an important photograph that should be placed in a particular section. Once you have your photos organized, you will be ready to purchase the scrapbooking supplies needed to begin.

What Supplies Do I Need?

The scrapbooking market is bursting with products. Some items are essential to have right away, others are wonderful decorating options, and many will just make scrapbooking a lot of fun.

BASIC SUPPLIES

Here are the basic supplies required to simply get your photographs in a safe place.

■ **An album** There are several styles of scrapbook albums available: three-ring binders and post-bound, spiral-bound, strap-hinged, and stitch-bound albums. Choose the highest-quality one that will suit your needs and budget.

Some factors to consider when choosing an album are these:

Is it made of materials that are safe for your photos?

Does it seem to be a durable album?

Can you add or remove pages if you desire?

Is its price manageable for your budget?

Does it lie flat when opened?

Can the pages be rearranged if you find you've left something out?

Are there protective covers available for the finished pages?

Are the page dimensions suitable for your needs?

■ **Refill pages** Most albums come with only a portion of the pages the album can actually hold. Refill packets are usually available where you purchase your album. It is wise to purchase all the pages you anticipate needing when you buy the album, in case the availability or style are affected by manufacturers.

If your budget is limited, you can start by purchasing only the refill pack of pages for the album you have chosen, saving up until it's a better time to invest in the album. Purchase pages made by a well-established company to help ensure the style will still be available when you are ready to buy the album itself. And be sure to protect the finished pages so they won't get soiled or bent while waiting to be inserted into the album.

■ **Protectors** Page protectors are plastic covers made to slide over or hold your completed scrapbook page in order to keep it clean and protected. Not all album styles have these available.

Here are some other basic supplies you will need:

■ **Regular scissors** for cropping photographs or for cutting decorative items for the pages
■ **T-square** for straight placement of the photos or for drawing caption lines
■ **Pencil** to make small dots that indicate photo placement or for drawing journaling lines
■ **White art eraser** to cleanly remove pencil marks
■ **Black pigment ink pen** for noting details in the captions and for journaling on the album pages
■ **Specially made photo-marking pen** to label any unmarked photos

- **Adhesives** for mounting your photographs, die cuts, or other decorative elements or photo corners
- **Your photographs and memorabilia**

THE EXTRAS

These extra supplies will help you decorate your pages.

- **Paper** in a variety of solid and patterned designs for backgrounds, mats, or accents
- **Die cuts** (precut paper shapes)
- **Stickers**
- **Paper cutter** to trim your photos or smaller papers
- **Templates** (shapes cut into a sheet of plastic to be used as a pattern for cutting a photograph, mat, or decorative element)

- **Decorative scissors** for cutting decorative edges for trimming photos, mats, or borders
- **Pens** in a variety of colors and tips
- **Decorative punches** for creating quick accents or elaborate scenes
- **Corner rounder** for softening the edges of your pictures and/or mat
- **Storage containers** to organize your supplies or for taking your supplies to workshops

THE RITZ

If you have these supplies, you'll use them!

- **Circle and oval cutters** to quickly cut an even, smooth shape
- **Stencils** for making designs and letters
- **Flexible curve** (a movable ruler used to form a curve of the flow you desire)
- **Craft knife**
- **Rubber stamps and pigment ink pads** to accent your page
- **Resource books** (quotations, child's picture dictionary, lettering books, and so forth)

These helpful tools will save time and give you creative options.

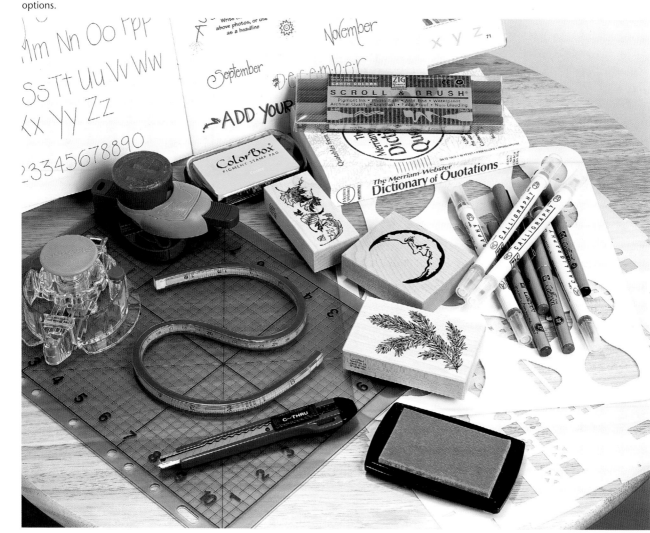

WORKSHOP: PLANNING YOUR ALBUM

GOAL Fine-tune what you want to include in your album.

ASSIGNMENT Create a list that will guide you in accomplishing your objectives.

STEPS List (or gather) the photographs you will probably want to include in this album. If it is a baby album, you might target events that occurred during the pregnancy and the birth through the first birthday. A wedding album might include the engagement pictures, bridal showers, and rehearsal dinner.

Consider how much information you will want to write to tell the story thoroughly.

Gather appropriate memorabilia.

Jot down other elements you might want to add—such as quotes, historical information, or other points of interest for the topic—so you don't forget to include them.

Decide what size album will be required to adequately hold the items and memorabilia you want to include.

Decide on the general tone you want to create (for example, festive, elegant, or old-fashioned).

Consider the style you want the pages to have.

Do you want to keep the pages simple or would you like to get really creative?

Once you have considered these options and gathered the things you are likely to include, keep the list in view in your work area. It needn't be set in stone if you get other inspirations and want to change direction, but it will help keep a target in mind that can provide consistency in the flow of your album.

Images

The most important images on your scrapbook pages will almost always be your photographs. They are typically the foundation of a scrapbook and will be a point of great interest to those who look through your albums. There are other images you will probably also make use of—memorabilia, die cuts, and other visual pieces you create for your page to enhance the details of the story. In this chapter we will consider primarily the photographic images.

The Power of Images

Every day, visual images impact and persuade. You are bombarded by fast-paced TV and movie clips and swayed by a thirty-second commercial or a magazine advertisement costing a company thousands of dollars to quickly induce you to buy their product.

Subtle, less manufactured images touch you all the time as you move about in your daily surroundings. Whether your environment is a large city with its opening-night galas, ethnic street markets, and busy subways, or a quiet small-town setting of familiar neighbors, church bake sales, and county fairs, you have around you a wonderful variety of sights that can inspire, move, or delight you.

Especially precious to you may be the photographic images you have of your family. You may have hundreds of pictures of family gatherings and activities and even a nice selection of old ones that have recorded for you the faces of your ancestors.

Selecting Photographs for Your Scrapbooks

You most likely possess more photographs than you will place in your scrapbooks. Each one captures a slightly different perspective of an event, yet a scrapbook is not just a compilation of photos. If you are adding journaling and some decorative elements, you will not have space to include all of the pictures from many activities. (However, I do encourage taking as many pages as you desire to chronicle an event, rather than always condensing the account into one or two pages.)

So, how do you select which pictures to use? There are always the obvious favorites. These are the photographs you know without question will be included on your album pages. Often they have wonderful colors and are focused perfectly, but sometimes they are selected because they portray a great expression or a classic moment you just couldn't leave out. Granted, the better our photographs, the nicer our page will look.

A scrapbook page usually comprises a representative selection of pictures. Choose ones that show the breadth of the activity—key people, places, and things of the event. For example, if the theme is a birthday party, you will want to include the guest of honor, the cake, presents (wrapped and opened), those who came to help celebrate, and any special decorations. Then include the whole room (catch the atmosphere) and some candid response photos (showing the fun). Try to primarily keep to those that are better photos in terms of color and focus, but be willing to include a less-than-great picture if it captures something special.

It is also possible to make a page with a grouping of many similar photos. These can successfully show a quick progression of moments, giving "movement" to the subject, as in the layout on the next page of Cade eating his first birthday cake.

On this two-page spread of Cade are pictures taken in rapid succession, working almost like a short movie clip when they were laid out on the page—showing the variety of expressions captured on his increasingly messy face. Other scenarios can work well in this manner. When my children were first walking, I occasionally followed closely with my camera while they wandered freely outside. I could quickly photograph the variety of their positions as they toddled around the yard exploring their environment. Pages I have made with these photos quickly return me to the day and the joy of observing their delight and fresh-eyed exploration.

Flower Child

Jackie and Lia

Eunice called me on the phone from next door. "Get the camera ready," she said. "Jackie just did Lia's hair!" I expected soft curls, but around the corner came this tiny reminder of the '60s. (There was a 4th flowered ponytail sticking straight out the back.) Thanks for the photo-op Jackie!

A group of pictures taken in rapid succession will work like a short movie clip when placed together.

Create an oversized visual or frame to support a single, special picture.

Create a visual scene with stickers or die cuts when you don't have a photo that shows the incident.

Occasionally a picture is so special that you may want to use it alone on a page. Even in a large album this can work. Create an oversized visual to suit it, and then frame the photo with a wide mat for emphasis.

Sometimes you may want to make a page telling a story for which you have no photographs. Create a page using other images as its core. Postcards or other memorabilia may be the focal point, but you can also create a visual scene by using large die cuts and/or stickers that help define the story.

This page describes a comic scenario that transpired when we were in the process of selecting yet another baby name. The large stickers were the inspiration for how the story could be symbolized in the album.

Nanniene's Gift

Scrapbooks are often described as a special vehicle by which a family is threaded together, the pieces in it working as patches of a lovely quilt of memories to pass on to the following generations. The scrapbook from Nanniene is a literal example of how this threading process can happen. Let me tell you the story from the beginning. . . .

It's Chicago, 1881. Baby girls are born to two neighboring families at 417 and 427 State Street. In a short time, little Elizabeth Hamilton Chew (Elise) and Nanniene Norton Thomasson, living just four doors apart, begin a friendship that would last over seventy years. A scrapbook, now belonging to Elise's granddaughter, invites us to catch a glimpse of these long-ago days. The album consists of thirty-one pages containing many pencil and watercolor images that illustrate neighborhood scenes, places visited, and surroundings fondly remembered of the shared moments and adventures of the two friends.

The girls, from somewhat prominent families, regularly shared their favorite activities. A tiny playhouse they called Little House was situated at the far end of the Thomasson's backyard. The girls spent leisure hours in this "playground" and mentioned hopscotch, roller-skating, and hoop rolling as favorite games they played. But Elise and Nanniene also went on excursions about the city in the "carryall with the fringe on top" in summer and on sleds pulled behind the family's carriage or sleigh in winter.

One entry, several pages in length, describes the day the girls took a picnic lunch up to the Chews' attic. The girls ate their lunch and then proceeded out onto the captain's walk with their opera glasses. Unknowingly, they had positioned themselves at precisely the right moment to view this scene: "For miles Lake Michigan could be seen and nothing higher than the water tower in sight to the south—but about two o'clock, the three Spanish boats were sighted coming from the north. The Pinta, Nina, and Santa Maria—and their destination, Columbian Exposition." The boats were crossing Lake Michigan to the Chicago port, where they would be anchored for the World's Fair in 1893. The girls were then twelve years old. The wonderful account continues. "That summer was never forgotten. Twice a week Mrs. Chew would take the girls to the World's Fair. Our favorite place was Streets of Cairo."

Throughout this slender scrapbook are two prominent themes—pickles and Fairy Day. Elise's Grandmother Meadowcroft was fondly remembered for the delicious pickles she made. Notations in this memory book tell us the girls toted these delicacies along on several outings to joyfully consume them. Even the crock that held them in the Chew home is described and illustrated. The pickles were apparently a regular treat.

And then there was Fairy Day. Perhaps you didn't know that May 1 is Fairy Day. This tradition, I presume, has never been widely celebrated, but it was a highlight of the year for these two imaginative little girls. And no wonder! Nanniene writes, "On May 1 Elise said all the fairies came out on that day and if you really wanted anything very much, you could always get it, if asked on that day!" Tales like that delight little girls! The years passed with both Elise and Nanniene marrying and raising their families in Maryland.

But I haven't yet told you why the book is a perfect example of threading generations together.

The pages of this scrapbook are the permanent dwelling place of five paper dolls wearing tiny fabric outfits lovingly crafted to accurate miniature detail. There is Grandmother Meadowcroft in her black dress and beaded India shawl, Dr. Chew in typical jacket and trousers, and Mrs. Chew in shirtwaist, long skirt, belt, and hanging bag. Several pages later is Elise Chew on the day she became Mrs. Theodore Forbes in April of 1906. She is beautifully adorned in a princess gown of soft white satin, lace trim from the real wedding dress, and tiny kid gloves. The last doll is Nanniene herself in the "airy looking gown" she wore in Elise's

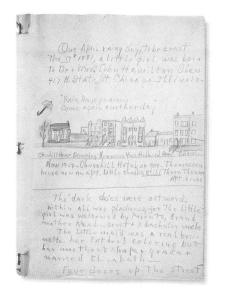

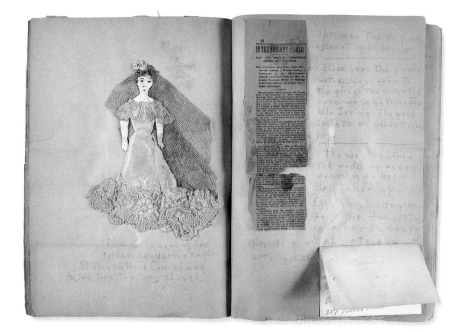

wedding—"white net over pink, carrying pink roses in leghorn hats tied up into a basket with broad pink ribbons." From the enclosed newspaper clipping of the event, these little outfits capture the gowns to the tiniest detail.

There I sat in 1999 on a lovely autumn afternoon, sharing lunch with Liz (Elizabeth Forbes Bowie) on the porch of her charming home. Brunette hair and chocolate-colored eyes set off her broad smile as we looked through the scrapbook and she reflected on the stories of her grandmother, the woman for whom she was named. She described her own daughter's excitement in looking through this album. "Emma was the one who discovered the tiny petticoats hidden within the layers of fabric that make up the little dresses." Was there any chance that Emma wouldn't feel a special bonding with these distant relatives? It was Emma's great-great-great-grandmother Meadowcroft who made the memorable pickles, her great-great-grandparents Dr. and Mrs. Chew who provided adventures for two little girls, and her great-grandmother Elise who was there for her to see and in some way experience.

Our story moves back to spring 1954. Elise's youngest child, Alice, was to be married on May 15. Nanniene had been thinking and planning for some time. She had carefully worked on a gift that was surely from her heart and full of her own childhood memories. Nanniene presented her gift to Alice, this delightful scrapbook titled Tales of Two Little Girls. The last page was considerably heavier than the others, for it was graced with a beautiful engraved silver pickle fork—the very gift that Mrs. Chew had given Nanniene for her wedding and the perfect symbol of the special friendship that Nanniene treasured.

What more could she want for Elise's only daughter than to wish her a life full of wonderful *memories like she has experienced? And it was destined to be, for Nanniene carefully timed the giving of this gift—exactly two weeks before Alice's wedding day. ". . . If you really wanted anything very much, you could always get it, if asked on that day!" Nanniene took no chances. This wonderful little album, pickle fork included, along with her best wishes for Alice's happy future, was presented on May 1—Fairy Day!*

The last shape worked well with one of the pictures in the layout on the next page.

Cropping

Once you select your photos, the next decision is how to use them to their best advantage. Here is where cropping comes into play. *Cropping* is the term used to describe any method of cutting your photograph. You can approach cropping in many ways, but you should do it for the purpose of enhancing the subject(s) and improving the layout. Sometimes you might do it just to remove a distracting element.

Consider cropping as the first frame of the picture. Choose a shape that helps the picture look its best. Unless you are cropping silhouette style, try to leave a fair amount of room around the subjects so they don't appear to be squeezed into the space.

CROPPING OPTIONS

Straight-cut a section. A small paper cutter is great for this.

Trim the corners into a smooth curve. This softens the look of the photo. If you like this, a corner rounder is a good investment.

Decorative scissors now come in many styles. You can use them to add a touch of design at the corners or to decorate the whole perimeter of the photograph. Use them cautiously if you are cutting the perimeter, as these add a lot of design, sometimes distracting the eye from the subjects in the photo.

Templates providing a variety of shapes and sizes are available for any look or theme. Using them as a pattern, mark the shape onto the photo, and then carefully cut along the lines.

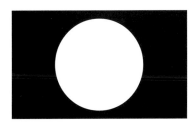

Silhouettes are achieved by cutting the subject out paper doll–style. You can use this method for a photograph with one person or a group. You can use it to create further interest and focus by cutting around an object (table, toy, and so on) that is an important feature in the photograph.

Make a two-in-one cut. For example, leave the bottom half of the photo untouched, but cut slightly into it partway up with the top of an oval or circle to frame the subject.

I keep my cropping relatively simple on most pages, normally choosing basic geometric shapes (squares, rectangles, circles, and generous ovals) and cutting the photos with straight-edged scissors. This seems to work most successfully. I sometimes use decorative scissors designs to enhance other parts of the page.

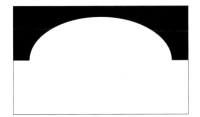

Some photos
will look great
when you crop
only the top
part into a
semicircle or
oval shape.

One day during that
visit we decided to try
to see the sun rise over
the ocean at the
Outer Banks...

We missed it
by a few crucial
minutes...

...but enjoyed a
glorious day!

Silhouette a
photo, and
then position it
coming out of a
large die cut.

1957

Laurie
Jayne
arrives

February 6

2 months old

7 months old

Howdy Doody
(on air '47-'60)
at popularity
peak.

President Eisenhower Formulates "Eisenhower Doctrine" For
Protection of Middle Eastern Nations from Communist Aggression
Gromyko Becomes U.S.S.R. Foreign Minister
"The Six" Sign Rome Treaty; Beginning of the Common Market
Britain Explodes Thermonuclear Bomb in Central Pacific
International Atomic Energy Agency Established
Teamsters Union is Expelled from AFL-CIO When Jimmy Hoffa
Refuses to Expel Criminals and Union Refuses to Expel Hoffa
Desegregation Crisis in Little Rock, Arkansas; President Eisenhower
Sends Paratroopers to Forestall Violence
U.S.S.R. Launches Sputnik I and II, First Earth Satellites

Marcia's 3rd Birthday

CROPPING TIPS

Cut neatly to keep edges smooth. When cutting curved shapes, feed the paper into the scissors, rather than moving your scissors around the paper, to achieve a smoother cut.

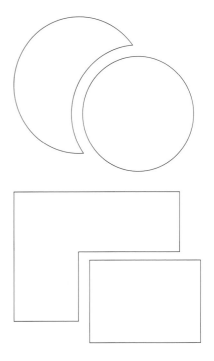

Think carefully before eliminating items like cars, appliances, or product containers (cereal boxes, and so on) that place this shot in a time frame. In just a few years these objects may evoke a bit of nostalgia.

Choose just a few different shapes. Having too many in one layout can be distracting.

Never crop a Polaroid picture. Air will get between the layers and break down the photograph. Instead, you can cut a frame out of paper and attach it to the front of the photo, covering the Polaroid border. You can easily decorate this frame with stickers, punched shapes, or ink designs and mount the entire piece on a second paper to create a double mat. Note: It is fine to crop Polaroid pictures taken with the older-style cameras available through the early seventies that had the throw-away negative, but don't cut your photo unless you're sure it was this kind!

Combine two pictures of a single (or similar) shape, one picture set into the other.

Cut images silhouette-style and make them look great coming out of an object related to your theme. A birthday cake, Easter egg, teacup, tulip, bathtub, swimming pool, baby buggy, or gift all work well.

What to Photograph

Once you begin scrapbooking, it is likely that your interest in snapping pictures and the elements you try to capture on film will expand. Let us consider how to make good use of the opportunity.

You can get a helpful perspective by looking at some old family photographs—those of previous generations or from your own childhood. Posed portraits have a place, but much more enjoyable are the pictures that show the spontaneous expressions and actions, typical surroundings, and interests of the people in them. They more clearly and colorfully describe the details of a particular life and personality. Any one photograph has the potential of catching a glimpse of a rarely seen side of a person's response to life.

I have several favorite photos from my childhood. One of them shows a Christmas gathering when I was about nine years old. My parents, my two sisters, and I had obviously been instructed to sit on my aunt's sofa for a family picture. There is my mother, a mannerly woman, comically sticking out her tongue at someone outside the lens's view. The picture perfectly captures the high-spirited get-togethers I remember.

One way to take meaningful pictures is to photograph people doing the things they love. We normally don't snap many shots of a family member engaged in their occupations and hobbies. Is it because we view the end product as more important than the process they enjoy so much? Or do we just forget to see it as special?

Perhaps through the years, your grandmother has knitted sweaters for the entire family. There's nothing unique here—you've all seen her spend hours at it. But wouldn't it be wonderful to have a photograph of her tenderly working on the tiny baby sweater she will soon nestle into a tissue-filled, ribbon-draped box to give to her first great-grandchild? And how much more valuable the image will be when the recipient of that gift unpacks from the cedar chest the carefully stored sweater for her own baby!

Your life is probably full of opportunities like this. Do you have any pictures of Dad at his place of employment? What about Mom carefully mixing together one of her fabulous trademark coffee cakes? Taking photographs of daily activities enables you to have images of how life typically is in an individual's or family's experience. I've realized that the things that occupy my family's schedule on a regular basis were those I often hadn't thought of capturing on film.

Maybe a child close to you is an avid reader or lovingly totes around a favorite toy. Have you taken any photos to capture it? The pastimes of children can be signs of what their careers will eventually be. It is wonderful to have a childhood photo that reveals those first seeds of interest.

Vary the Perspective

Another consideration is how you capture the scope of these moments. It is advantageous to photograph the activity in a variety of ways. Take a picture that shows the room where someone is working. Another can be a closer perspective of the person and the tools he uses. Still another might be a close-up, with details of his hands and revealing the textures of the materials with which he is working.

Photograph from a variety of angles as well. Take some group shots—posed and spontaneous. Try to get close-ups of faces, revealing the emotions that permeate the event. Action shots pull the viewer into the photo, allowing participation in the moment and a share in the fun, effort, or victory. For outdoor activities, take some faraway pictures of the landscape, letting a viewer later understand how the environment and weather may have affected the day.

Be cautious of the mind-set of posing your subjects. It typically requires stopping the natural activity so everyone can face a camera, interrupting the moment that would make a better photograph. An exception is a photo to note who was there, for example, as a group shot at a family reunion. Try to take it at the beginning or the end of the activity, but in the middle, just let the shutter snap away!

The objects in your pictures can add immense interest to the photograph and are powerful vehicles that can quickly surface memories of that time. Unwrapped toys in a birthday or Christmas photo, the rooms you live in (with their current furniture and color schemes), product packaging, and cars (the exteriors *and* interiors) make for great reminiscing. Listen to a group of siblings looking through a box of photos from their childhood. The stories will begin to flow as they remember details triggered by viewing these objects. The out-of-style clothing and hairstyles only add to the fun!

Especially interesting are appliances and other markers of technological development. You may be so used to your own environment that you might not

4

The Magic of Memorabilia

$\mathcal{M}$any pieces of my ancestors' lives remain—furniture, linens, dishes and kitchen utensils, recipes, and photographs. We knew these items existed. They were the things we had seen surrounding our grandparents and that made their houses into homes. They were also the things we associated with many specific memories of the times we had shared. But eventually the family said our good-byes to the last of these cherished parents and grandparents and placed them in their final resting places. In the days that followed we all gathered and began the task of sorting through and sharing the possessions that remained. But just as a person has inner, less-seen parts of their beings, so too, can a home hold some surprises.

Belongings That Connect Us

After Grandma passed away, we found within some small boxes various relics of her and Grandpa's life together and mementos she had saved from the belongings of previous generations. Such things are called *memorabilia* because of the strong memories they stir in those who save them; for later generations, memorabilia are tangible parts of ancestors' lives that give insights into how they lived. Saved family memorabilia bonds us to our ancestors, as we hold and touch the same items that they held and used.

Enhance a family album by including items of historical significance on its pages.

In our family, a few of the treasures that survived are a December 1882 tax receipt (from the same county I live in) issued to my great-great-grandfather Levi Finical for the sum of $3.81, numerous schoolbooks, titled "souvenir," noting the grade levels of several relatives who were educated in one-room schoolhouses in the early 1900s, a 1912 gas and fuel bill (charging $1.50 *for the month*!), a story-book from Grandma's early childhood titled *Dolly at the Seaside*, the 1946 Kennel Club registration for Grandpa's beagle, and various postcards and newspaper clippings. It makes me curious, when finding things like these, about what prompted someone to save *these* tokens when thousands of similar items flowed through their lives and were disposed of along the way.

Now safely tucked into our family scrapbook are a few of the rationing coupons issued to my grandparents during World War II. Memorabilia clearly gives our albums a historical dimension. Seeing pieces from my family's past reminds me of the value that the things around me can later hold and encourages me to place some mementos in our scrapbooks alongside the photos and written record of my family's activities.

Indeed, we call these albums *scrapbooks* because they have typically held varying scraps that have been deemed important or interesting in some way. These pieces can help define the historical time period. They are not only the props that supported the event (like programs and ticket stubs) but are often examples of artistry and design of the time as well.

Plenty of Possibilities

Thousands of things are available that you could use in your scrapbooks. Most feasible to include are paper items because they are flat, readily available, a key part of the stuff you might save from most events, and easy to work with. You might also use three-dimensional pieces that are relatively thin.

Jenna drew a telling picture of herself with chicken pox (on page 33). Seeing it in her scrapbook will surely remind her of those polka-dotted days.

Among the obvious items you might save that you could put in your scrapbooks are invitations, party napkins, greeting cards, postcards, letters, newspaper clippings, and locks from a baby's first haircut. Also easy to include are airline tickets, luggage tags, brochures, itineraries, maps, menus, flattened pennies from the imprinting machines at zoos or theme parks, recipes, product packaging, postage stamps, fabric scraps, matchbook covers, theater playbills, campaign buttons, bumper stickers, cloth-embroidered patches or badges, hotel keys, receipts, price tags, shopping bag emblems, subway tickets or tokens, small drink umbrellas, wrist bracelets from theme parks or hospital stays, and even tiny baby bonnets. School souvenirs to include are varsity letters; ribbon from homecoming corsages; awards, certificates, or ribbons; pieces of championship basketball nets; sheet music; grade cards; and good reports from teachers. The list could go on and on.

In 1942 my dad and uncle (who were then eighteen and twenty years old, respectively) decided to take a train trip west before their service in World War II started. Fortunately, a postcard they sent home to their parents was kept through the years. That souvenir and the two photos that were taken during that vacation make a fun scrapbook page that captures the time and their message. Placing it on a map motif further emphasizes the point of the page.

In another example of including memorabilia on scrapbook pages, Thelma was making scrapbooks for each of her grandchildren. One of the pieces of memorabilia

Incorporate children's art-work into their scrapbooks to preserve a glimpse of their perspective.

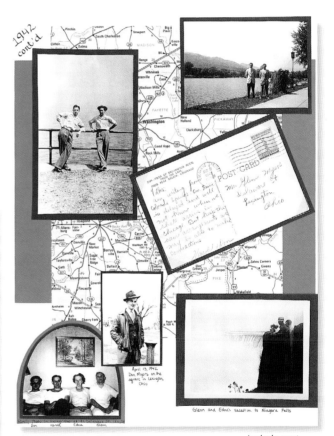

Include post-cards that have survived with photographs from the same time frame.

she included in Laura's album was a pretty handkerchief. Ever since Laura was little, she had preferred using a soft cloth hanky to a paper tissue. Thelma had purchased decorative children's hankies for her, which Laura kept folded in her dresser drawers and under her pillow. Thelma's Aunt Eileen had also had a fondness for pretty handkerchiefs. Writing this similarity in the scrapbook brought a tangible link between these two family members of distant generations.

Sara

I bumped into the dark-haired woman on a picture-perfect morning in July.

Children and puppies darted excitedly around the transformed Georgetown parking lot, tugging at the arms of distracted grown-ups and weaving them through rows of colorful flea market booths. A cool breeze tried to revive some of the tired merchandise—Oriental rugs, overstuffed chairs, and togs that hadn't hugged a body in decades. Meanwhile sun and shade danced harmoniously, bringing to notice the unique details of each piece of mismatched dishware and furniture and the tools of many trades. Boxes of gritty hardware were next-door neighbors to shelves of books and trays heaped with luscious produce. Everyone had come with hopes of spotting a treasure and taking it home at a bargain price.

That's where Sara and I met. She was quietly occupying a small wooden chair when I came around the corner. Her heart-shaped face framed blue eyes and smiling lips. Some people share themselves easily. Sara was one of them.

I quickly learned about her tiny hometown in Georgia, a summer romance with Alton, and her graduation from the women's college in Milledgeville. I even learned that her dad affectionately called her Duckie. She was a sentimental gal who obviously enjoyed the tiny details of her life.

But Sara was not there in the flesh. I met her within the pages of the scrapbook she had made during her senior year of college beginning in the fall of 1925. Of course, I took Sara home with me.

Telling you how I met her is one thing; trying to describe her album is an entirely different matter. I've seen hundreds of memory books, but never one with the surprising treasures this one holds. It includes letters and invitations and programs from various activities. Coupled with them is an unusual entry—a Coca-Cola bottle cap attached to a long piece of string. The message next to it reads, "Tried to attract Frances Howell Dill's attention down in 102 by flipping this on her window one night during study hall."

"Never will forget that party. . . . I went as Bill's sweetheart in the attire of a sheik. . . . Had the grandest time I ever did have." Not only are the invitation, napkin, and party favors here, so are two small toys she won that Valentine's Day evening. The molded pink baby doll and now-indented (though once regal-looking) plastic lion keep each other company in her book. Apparently, bulk was not an issue for Sara. When

closed, the book's right side is at least twice as thick as its spine, so stuffed it is with all her treasures.

Crepe paper and satin ribbon spill from the pages. They are decorations she carried off after college events, happily heading back to her room with the booty. The tangled wad of string with which she learned to make "crow's feet" is dated Sunday, October 4. A pencil stub sharpened to its last breath of life includes a notation reading "Phillip Warren gave this to me when I was in ninth grade."

My favorite entry is a now paper-thin, shriveled crescent labeled "Mr. Shealey gave me my first tangerine." Surely tasting its juicy sweetness for the first time was a memorable experience, but I am still delighted by the image every time I think of her taping a piece of it in her scrapbook. Sara Fay Reid apparently saved everything!

I don't recommend making an album this way. Several pages are greatly damaged from the still-wrapped chewing gum, corsages, and *candy held within its pages, and overfilling it has been hard on its con-struction. I am, however, totally charmed by this scrapbook.*

I'm also saddened that it has wandered into hands outside Sara's family. How unfortunate that her great-grandchildren or distant nieces and nephews aren't the ones now enjoying this unique piece of history. It is their history! But it is a piece of my history, too. Sara's album is a wonderful example of Americana that depicts the daily activities of an individual and chronicles that year of my country's story in vivid per-sonal details that a textbook rarely includes.

An example is one treasure pinned to the corner of a letter Sara received from her sister, Ethel. Her handwriting tells the story: "Sara, I am sending you something for your scrapbook. Eddie Rivers, who is in Pennsylvania, went out to see the wreck of the Shenandoah *and sent the Drug Store a whole lot of Kodak pictures of it, and a piece of the outer covering—and I cut off a little piece to send you." Here it is, still in her album—a tiny silver rectangle of aluminum-painted fabric once part of a famous dirigible that fell from a stormy sky in three broken pieces, killing fourteen. The Ohio tragedy saddened the nation as news of it spread on a September day in 1925. This remnant is a bit of America's story, and now I am its guardian. Yes, I'm happy to be this album's adop-tive family. Sara, I will take good care of you.*

Some of the mementos I have saved in scrapbooks are a grocery receipt from the month Lia was born, paper snowflakes we cut one wintry day, a small WELCOME HOME sign that awaited us when I came home from the hospital with Kyle made by his older siblings, a pair of chopsticks from a memorable dinner out, an empty sugar packet that bears the face of Richard Nixon, several pertinent comic strips, a story written by my sister when she was in third grade, a potty-training chart cov-ered with the stickers of success, letters to Santa, party hats, and even an original black-and-white-striped Barbie bathing suit. Each has added a stroke of nostalgia to its page.

Working with Memorabilia

You can work with memorabilia in much the same way you do your photographs, trimming when necessary (or advantageous) and matting the items to help the color and balance of the pages. Cut brochures apart, placing various images and/or descriptive paragraphs from them alongside your own photographs and journal-ing, or assemble them collage-style. Like old suitcases plastered with the names of cities visited, your scrapbook pages can hold clipped-paper souvenirs that capture the highlights of a trip or other activity.

But what can you do with more bulky memorabilia? My neighbor Melissa had that problem arise. She had attended an art camp and came home with samples of various types of work she had done—watercolor, charcoal, and pottery. Most of the paper items were too large to consider placing in her album; the pottery obviously wasn't even an option. Melissa decided to set them all up in an attractive way and photograph the art pieces together as a still life. It was a lovely way to have the images in her book. They were, after all, her expressions of the lessons learned that year—an important part of her art camp experience.

Melissa solved another dilemma efficiently. She had served as a junior staff member at a conference for Japanese students. The staff had been given daily schedules of the specific activities for each day. She wanted to include these in her scrapbook but didn't want to consume too much space. Taking them to a copy center, Melissa reduced each page to its smallest easily readable size (about two inches by three inches in this case). They were then feasibly placed with the photos of that week. How wonderful to include the actual information in its original format—without having to write it all out. (Also see Appendix, "Product Safety Basics.")

Adding Memorabilia Safely

You need to take a bit of care to include memorabilia in your scrapbook without sacrificing the safety of your photographs. Most of the memorabilia you place there will probably be made of paper. Here are some things to keep in mind when including them.

Many kinds of paper contain ingredients that are harmful to the longevity of the photographs you are placing in your album. These ingredients can cause discoloration, often yellowing the photograph quickly. Acid is the primary concern; it is often present in paper products and can damage photographs. The acid can also migrate, causing a chemical reaction with other paper, with the photographs on the page, or with other items elsewhere in your album within close proximity. (See Appendix, "What Is Photo-Safe?") There are pH-testing pens that will indicate whether or not the paper contains acid, but they will leave a permanent mark on the area tested. To be on the safe side, assume the paper has ingredients that will harm your photos and use any of the following methods to protect your photograph: place it on buffered paper (if you are using page protectors, too), enclose it in photo-safe plastic, treat it with a deacidification spray, or photocopy it onto acid-free paper (and use the photocopy in your album instead of the original).

BUFFERED PAPER

Many papers are now manufactured with a buffering agent that neutralizes acid; these are called *buffered papers*. There are even papers with a buffering "reserve"— an added amount of the buffering agent to keep the paper from reverting to an acidic pH over time. Memorabilia can be placed on a piece of buffered paper in order to prevent the acid from spreading to photographs or other papers on that page. Some archivists suggest that buffered paper shouldn't touch the front of a color photograph, as on a facing page, for example; they suspect that the buffering agent will gradually eat away the emulsion (top layer) of the picture. If your album pages or decorative paper are buffered, it is important that you use page protectors to shield photographs on facing pages. Then, when the scrapbook is closed, the buffered paper will not have contact with your photographs.

ENCLOSURES

Another way to include memorabilia is to place it in a photo-safe plastic envelope. Various sizes of envelopes are available. Simply purchase the correct size, insert the memorabilia in the envelope, and secure it to your album page.

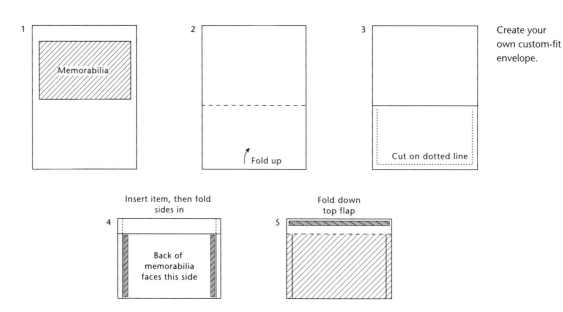

Create your own custom-fit envelope.

Neatly enclose memorabilia for safety, and then add it to your layout.

You can also customize an envelope that will perfectly fit memorabilia by using photo-safe plastic (see Appendix) and a roll of photo-safe transparent tape. Cut a piece of plastic twice as long plus one inch, and one inch wider than the item you will be enclosing. Fold the plastic, creating the bottom of the envelope (see illustration, above). Trim about one-quarter inch from each of the remaining three sides of what will be the back of the envelope (see illustration, above). Place the tape along the edge of the two sides of the back and fold over the excess tape from the front, sealing tight. Insert the memorabilia, and then close the top as you did the sides. Use the tape to attach the envelope to the page. This method works well for any item that needs to be seen from the front only. For postcards, letters, and anything else you want to be able to take out and read, leave one side open to enable slipping it in and out.

DEACIDIFICATION SPRAY

It isn't unusual these days for some common paper items (greeting cards, for example) to be acid-free. But if these papers, or any of your older memorabilia, test acidic with a pH-testing pen, another option is to treat them with a deacidification product before including them in your album. Deacidification products allow you to neutralize the acids in the paper. Follow the directions on the product for adequate results.

PHOTOCOPIES

A problem that scrapbookers frequently encounter is how to include newspaper clippings in albums. This is one case where it is advisable *not* to use an authentic item in your album. Daily newspapers are printed on very low-quality paper that is highly acidic and that yellows quickly. One way to use a clipping is to photocopy it onto acid-free paper, a definite step up in durability.

Any memorabilia you include in your scrapbook will add much to the account for other generations to enjoy in the years to come.

WORKSHOP: MEMORABILIA

GOAL   Practice ways of including memorabilia safely in your album.

ASSIGNMENT   Adapt the format of a memento that in its current form is not suitable to include in a scrapbook.

STEPS   Choose a piece of memorabilia that is an important piece to one of your stories.
Consider ways you might capture it in a usable two-dimensional format: photograph it, reduce, enlarge, or repeat the design on a copier. Use these reproductions as a primary image on the page or as a border, mat, or background element.
Incorporate other photos and suitably sized memorabilia onto the layout.
Add journaling to complete your page.

Use your most successful effort with your photos and journaling to create a page depicting the activity or event.

May 2 18/43 Elderton Pa
Dear Charles Hazell and all the rest Just got home from church - had fresh fish for Dinner I Hope every one well out there we are all fine here too, had a few weeks been pretty busy, had the paper Hanger for ... House ... every Thing white down stairs she got very tired by spells, and I made Mahala three and have a good dress too make for Mahala this week and also made her five new aprons, my self two new aprons, and have too make Jean a long Dress this week ... night and ... muslin night ... aprons ... and took a ... made them ... wear as long ... very well ... nicely ... and ... for her ... too work too ... Keeps a going ... Helen Altman was getting Married Friday we herd but havent ... i.e. ...

Mr. and Mrs. Charles Altman
Mansfield Ohio
R 3 ... So. Diamond St.

AIR MAIL

Thank you Thank you Thank you Thank you
I lo... I never ...

You dont write my hearts be Johansen on a major de here arou and whe two b grapes b oed hide WA H

Dear ... is dele yesterda long. n all h hom W hope a sleep up too

This ... row before went ... wheel ... and we ... it to Have We werent desperate on ... to see if they could get ... Sharp your dads bad all ... figures ready on income ta... f... the nice presents. Love Grandma

Words to Preserve in
Your Scrapbooks

*W*e've all heard the familiar saying, "A picture is worth a thousand words." Occasionally a photograph is so good that it may well be that descriptive. Most photos, however, share with us tiny glimpses of a moment, leaving us with more questions about the story than answers.

Learning About My Great-Grandmother

Let me tell you about my great-grandmother. She was born Anna Mary Manges on June 26, 1867, married Francis George Altman on February 28, 1889, in Indiana, Pennsylvania, and had ten children (the ninth being Charles, my grandfather).

Here is a picture of her sitting on a porch swing at the family farm. The photograph was taken in 1947 at a gathering for her eightieth birthday celebration. The image shows me what she looked like—her approximate height, build, coloring, and facial features. Without this photograph, I probably wouldn't know these physical details. I am happy I have it—it links me to her in a small way.

But one day, I came across this letter (the top letter on the previous page) she had sent to her son and his wife (my grandparents) in Ohio. She was seventy-five years old at the time. The letter isn't fancy; it's simply a greeting to them from her neighboring state, and it shares a bit of her visit to another son and daughter-in-law's home.

"I made Mahala three every day dresses since I came to Franks and have a good dress too make for Mahala this week and allso made her five new aprons, my self two new aprons, and have too make Jean a long Dress this week for an exercise

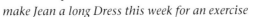

at colligue till Fri night and allso Frank two muslin night gowns and mother Held four aprons besides what other I done I had made Ethell three aprons and took a part two dresses for her and made them smaller for her. . . ."

Even though my great-grandmother's spelling and grammar are a bit of an obstacle, her letter has done an amazing thing. Suddenly I can see her in my mind's eye, active—doing things. I am also able (because of the photograph) to envision how a person of her physical makeup and age would move about doing these activities. I picture her busily going from job to job in the chores of those days, actually stitching the fabric into all those garments. It's like a mini film clip in my mind. My great-grandmother (who passed away eight years before I was born) has suddenly become alive to me.

I can also detect a little of her view of life from her relating of these activities. I notice that the letter is devoid of any tone of complaint. Apparently, she was happy to employ her skill for the benefit of her family and extended family. (Mother Held, whom she mentioned, was her daughter-in-law's mother.) I like knowing that my great-grandmother was a kind woman who cared in practical ways when there was a need. Clearly, words enable scrapbookers to share in a faraway moment.

The way you approach describing a subject and the skill levels you have to do it are less important than being sure you get it said. Please, please, write your stories! The text needn't be in flowing paragraphs. Use whatever space you need to fill in the details that you aren't communicating in other ways. Stop and think of exactly what it is you want to share, being less concerned with producing a great piece of writing than with the goal of making sure your family knows what happened. Let's not be a generation that so easily neglects the written record of our family history, simply because we think photographs alone will do the job of clearly capturing our lives for our descendants.

RECORDING YOUR GOOD-BYES

Dad's funeral had taken place that morning—a tearful good-bye we shared with family and friends that was punctuated with the twenty-one-gun salute in honor of his years of service during World War II. A short time later, many of the sympathy bouquets that had been delivered to the funeral home were transported to the cemetery. We returned to the burial site that afternoon. That's when my sister came up with a lovely idea.

Marcia began gently pulling the flowers out of the arrangements, grouping them by color. She and our younger sister, Laurie, then covered Dad's entire grave with them in a fragrant spread reminiscent of a quilt. My children also helped place blooms here and there, a way for them to say a final good-bye to their grandpa. It was a beautiful tribute to Dad—the flowers sent with love from family and his many friends placed over him in one huge bouquet. For us, it was a final gesture of care for this man who had always looked out for us so well.

Making a page to represent that afternoon was comforting to me. The photographs and journaling recorded how various members of our family worked together to help each other make it through a difficult day.

Wonderful Resources at Hand

Perhaps you remember your grand-mother quietly singing little songs as she went about weeding the garden. Maybe she taught you these when you were a child, or your young mind learned them simply by hearing them again and again as you worked along-side her. What were the lyrics that spilled from her lips, filling the air as she patiently coaxed the vegetables to maturity? What was the phrase, embroidered in colorful letters, that hung on her kitchen wall? I suppose your children have presented you with crayoned masterpieces, the lavish crin-kled offerings of their love and affec-tion joyfully spilled onto paper in large, misshapen letters. From these, you can pull words that will grace your scrapbook pages with meaningful parts of your experiences and relationships. Or you can include the originals or photo-copied versions. There is a bounty of material from which to choose.

Consider the family favorites first. Are there books, songs, sayings, or quotes that were a special part of your family experience or geographic background? You might have storybooks that were important in your early childhood. Perhaps your grandfather's hero was a political figure. Adding a phrase from one of his speeches onto a page that depicts your grandfather may help define the essence of the man. Add another nostalgic touch by including names of pertinent places where your family members have worked or played at different times in their lives. Explain the details in your notations.

Love Letters

The early history of many families includes love letters written back and forth by a smitten couple. These tender messages portray not only the beloved but the writer as well. Later, the family trove was blessed with little ones who, when they were big enough to take crayon in hand, began expressing their own affection to their parents. Ah, love letters. Little else warms the heart like these unsolicited offerings. Words from them can communicate the foundational warmth and care of your family to the next generation.

Of course, what counts as a love letter can have many styles: the expected flowery prose but also a grateful note of thanks or a silly cartoon drawing.

A series of ten cards and notes written by my daughter Jacie began arriving in the mail near Mother's Day during her freshman year of college. Each was cleverly penned with a message to me that reflected the artwork from the stationery on which she had written it. I was struck by her thoughtfulness and the time it took

The Legend of the Tooth Fairy

Saturday night, February 5, 2000, Jenna pulled her 2nd baby tooth out. It had been wiggly a long time!

The next morning Daddy insisted that the Tooth Fairy was a man, not a woman. I guess he was right ..

Now we have proof!

for her to make such a gesture. Some of the cards were sweet; a few made me laugh; but all of them warmed my heart. Beyond the kind words she wrote, I was touched by the evidence they were of whom *she* had become— a caring, expressive, articulate, and fun young woman. These letters will always be among my most precious possessions.

Any handwritten letters, postcards, or notes by family members can serve as meaningful tidbits to include in your album. You can photocopy the letter (enlarging or reducing it if necessary) and cut out sections of the copy to use as a border, background, or even a wide mat for a photo. How about using a copy of someone's signature

Just for fun, make a page describing a silly family incident. (Thanks, John! You're a sport!)

Children often surprise us with their innocent wisdom. Record these pearls as titles or borders on a page.

"FRIENDS ARE GOOD FOR YOUR HEALTH"
ALEX - AGE 8½

under their own picture? You can also use this with a child's school picture showing his or her handwriting that year. The written account of a family story that was repeatedly told by your Auntie Maude can add warmth and roots to your album, as can the surprisingly wise (and often comic) philosophies of your children.

There are many other words we can incorporate into our scrapbooks. Book titles, TV show titles or their theme songs, advertising slogans and jingles, children's poems or nursery rhymes, slang words and phrases from any era, headlines from the newspaper, and quotes from just about anywhere can add just the right touch to emphasize the theme of a page.

Sometimes you may have a selection of random pictures that you want to include in your scrapbook, yet they don't necessarily fit together in any theme or time frame. Connect them with a little bit of clever wording or an appropriate quote.

A child's letter to Santa can be the key element of a page that also ties in other activities of the holiday celebration that year.

Thomas Jefferson's Commonplace Books

Life was operating at a brisk pace—meetings to attend, decisions to make, papers and speeches to write, and always a pile of correspondence waiting to be processed. He was a man of influence and fame, yet here he was quietly working again on this varied compilation. He had thoughtfully read, chosen, cut, and saved newspaper articles that interested him in some way. Now he sat at his desk, his analytical eye and methodical ways apparent as he put these papers he deemed important in order.

Life had held some difficult moments of late. Not everyone appreciated or agreed with some of the ways he handled his responsibilities. Even some of his most personal moments were under scrutiny. His public stoicism following the death of his daughter Maria was observed, analyzed, and criticized by some. She was only twenty-five years old. The loss was the most recent in a long string of deaths that had robbed him of someone dear.

Yet it was not in the activities and interaction with his peers that he would reveal some of his most private thoughts. No, these emotions he held more guardedly. But in these quiet moments, when he read and reread poems whose subjects were other girls named Maria, he could respond to his grief at losing her. The clippings each reflected his thoughts in some way. This one was an expression of the immense sadness he experienced at her untimely death:

> *Thou ling'ring star with less'ning ray,*
> *Thou lov'st to greet the early morn.*
> *Again thou usher'st in the day*
> *My Mary from my soul was torn.*

This man who had already made such an impact on his young nation, this Thomas Jefferson, sat remembering her at his desk in the President's House (later known as the White House), the poem's lines surely connecting with his grieving heart. Yes, this one, too, would be pasted in his book.

It appears that the scene described is more than speculation. One of his volumes contains a letter tucked inside the front cover:

Com: University Library.

Gentlemen,
Mr. Jefferson left in his library two scrap books, which, it is said were compiled by his own hands during the term of his political administration. One of these antique volumes was presented to Mr. Ewd. R. Chambers of Mecklenburg Va, and, by him to me some years since. I propose to place the same at the disposal of the proper authorities of the University Library. If in their judgment it shall be deemed worthy a position among the relicks of its supposed author, I shall be gratified at its acceptance.

Respectfully, Yrs. &.
A. T. Laird
Staunton Va.
April 8th 1851

One of Thomas Jefferson's scrapbooks contains a pressed leaf thought to be connected to an agreement he made with a dear friend.

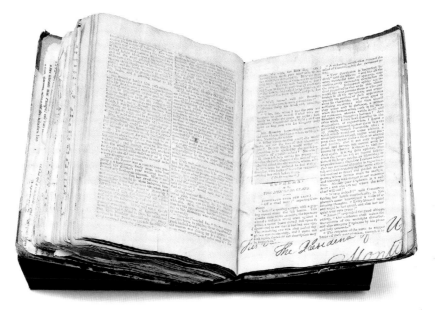

Many pages in Jefferson's scrapbooks are made on envelopes from correspondence he received during his presidency.

Four scrapbooks are now the possessions of the University of Virginia library. They are identical in style, format, and appearance, clearly indicating the same person compiled them all. Thomas Jefferson had long been in the habit of transferring material into books of his own, typically handwritten transcripts into what were called commonplace books. *As the demands on his time increased, his approach changed from handwriting the text to the more efficient system of clipping articles and pasting them onto a page. The method served him well.*

The articles included in his scrapbooks cover a broad variety of topics that certainly fit the man while offering us a few surprises. The sections are arranged by topic, including political comments and details of Fourth of July anniversaries—how they were celebrated in various cities and the toasts that were made to Jefferson, George Washington, and other prominent figures. Literary pieces, agriculture, home building and maintenance, and medical information are other subjects included. There are

Of course, you will also be chronicling the events and captioning the photos themselves. Here are the key pieces of information to include in your scrapbook journaling:

Who: Who was there or was the guest of honor? Definitely include who is in the photo!

What: What is this photo telling about the person or event? Is it obvious without words?

When: When did it take place? Record month, day, and year!

Where: What is the location of the activity? Names of places and specific addresses are interesting and helpful.

Why: Identify the occasion.

Use these pieces of information as titles or in the captions of the photos. Next you want to expand the basics and tell more of the story.

Enhance your journaling by remembering the emotions triggered by the occasion or that made the day memorable in some other way. What comes to mind when you see the snapshots? What did you feel and think during the event? Describe memorable sights, sounds, smells, tastes, or textures. It's not just the facts but the ways they impacted you that make the reading interesting. By colorfully telling the story, you invite the reader to be a guest at the event.

If possible, get some other perspectives of the day. Everyone sees things from their own viewpoint. Someone else who shared in the day may add some great details that you didn't observe.

Write down specific thoughts and feelings regarding the event.

JOURNALING TIPS

It may be helpful to jot the story down on a spare piece of paper before you put it on your scrapbook page. There are a couple of reasons for this. Your initial instincts may miss some important details. A rough draft will help you work out the kinks and ensure that you include the important information. Also, you will be able to determine the amount of space required to tell it. Do this before you get too far into the planning of your page lay-out. With your first draft and photos in hand, you will know the space available to give to decorative aspects of the page.

Try to be clear (give precise details), correct (give accurate information), concise (use words well), kind (avoid recording anything that would embarrass someone), and thor-ough (fill in the details to paint the picture for your reader).

Handle journaling point of view in any of the following ways, but keep consistent throughout the album so it's less confusing for the reader. Consider these captions for a snapshot of Joshua playing in a mud puddle:

First person: "I'm a messy boy!"
Second person: "You're a messy boy!"
Third person: "Joshua is a messy boy!"

Always include the full names of anyone who is not an immediate family member. If that person is a prominent part of the book, you needn't do this with every picture.

Over time, family expressions or phrases may be lost if people slip out of the habit of using them. If your family has some (and most do), write them down and if possible explain how they originated.

At the page's edge or another inconspicuous place, write your name and the date you made the page. Be sure to write it in a way that doesn't confuse the date with that of the event. If the pages you purchase have a built-in sturdy edge, this is a great place to write it. Noting this will add a nice touch of detail and tell your family that you recorded the story on that particular day.

When captioning a group shot, use a centered dot rather than a comma for a tidier look and easier reading.

The main complaint of most scrapbookers regarding journaling is that they don't like their handwriting. I think it's important for you to include your own handwriting in the album. It doesn't have to be fancy to look good. The key factor in attractive penmanship is consistency in the size, shape, and angle of the letters. Basic first-grade ball-and-stick letters are great! If you need to, practice to improve your skill. To achieve even-sized let-ters that are larger than my standard writing, I often draw three lightly penciled lines (like those on elementary school paper) for each row of writing and pencil in the words before I finish them in ink. It takes a few more minutes, but I am much happier with the results.

Capture the Family

An easy way to make quick work of collecting some specifics on all the living members of your family is to build an album with a two-page spread for each rela-tive. Compile a survey of about twenty to thirty questions that would provide interesting information about your family. Use the same survey for everyone. The answers to these questions combined with a few photos from various stages of each of their lives make a delightful account. Compilations of this nature allow you to notice more clearly the threads that run through the family line. It is another way to link you and stir your affection for one another.

Here are some ideas for questions your survey could include:

Full given name

Full name of parents

Names of all siblings

Nicknames

Date and place of birth

Occupations I've had

Hobbies

A childhood memory

Family pets (type, pet's name, and description)

Favorite childhood toy

Favorite food

Favorite colors

Best gift I ever received

An influential person in my life

An influential moment in my life

My passion is . . .

U.S. president in the year of my birth

A pet peeve of mine

A funny habit I have

Favorite saying or quote I use

Something unusual I've done

An embarrassing moment

I'm most proud of . . .

What I've learned in life

One bit of wisdom to pass on

My favorite job

First car

The most important day in my life

What I'd like to be remembered for

Description of a normal day at various times in my life

Something I've always wanted to do

Three of my goals in life have been . . .

Three favorite stories from my life

Think about the kind of questions you would like to answer. You can tailor the survey by including items that will pertain specifically to your family (for example, "Age I began working in the family business" or "My favorite memory from our summers at Buckeye Lake"). Encourage your family members to respond to the survey as thoroughly as they desire. Have a parent fill out the form for any baby in the family to make a humorous page. Have various relatives fill in the details they know about the lives of deceased family members to create a more complete family record.

Sometimes it may work better to visit and interview a relative rather than to have him or her answer the questions on paper. If tape-recording (or videotaping) the conversation is acceptable to all parties involved, you may be the recipient of even more details than your relative would have written for you, and you will have captured his or her voice as well.

Assemble the album in any manner you like. Attach each survey sheet directly onto the scrapbook page (so each person's own handwriting can be seen), or use the pieces of information to make a more creative presentation from your relatives' responses. Journal the answers around the border of the page or around individual pictures. Translate other parts to paragraph form.

You may get lucky and have a few relatives who dive into this project, writing down pages and pages of wonderful memories they have. I hope this project will produce loads of interesting details you may never have known that describe your family in full color and action. Think of the fun that a great-grandchild could have in years to come, pulling an album containing such material from the shelf and discovering the uniqueness of his or her family's heritage. You have the opportunity to make that possible.

WORKSHOP: WORDS

GOAL Paint a picture of a scene with words.

ASSIGNMENT Write a few paragraphs describing the details surrounding a favorite photo you have taken. Assume that the reader of your album was not present when the photo was taken. How can you describe the setting for him or her?

STEPS Look at the picture, letting your mind wander back to that moment. Try to recapture the mood and as many details as you can. Consider sights, sounds, smells, textures, moods, and even the weather.

Get these things on paper.

When you've exhausted the possibilities, begin to organize your thoughts into an order that will read well.

Correct any grammar or spelling errors.

Transfer the descriptions onto the page; your account will allow your family to understand the event and why it was meaningful.

6

Laying Out a Scrapbook Page

*Y*ou've just picked up a new packet of pictures, and they look great! In most of them the color is bright, everyone is in focus, and you managed to get on film the most important moments. How do you create from these a successful scrapbook page—one that really communicates the activity and fills in any gaps?

Perhaps you are working from a box of childhood photos and have six or eight from Christmas 1967. Or maybe it is an old tin filled with images of grandparents and great-grandparents that will begin your album. How you approach getting them nicely on the page will be the same.

Making a scrapbook page causes you to decide what to communicate about the person, activity, or event that is your theme and how much space to give to each aspect. You will point the reader in a direction, painting in the details in various ways and sharing the special things you want the reader to know. That is the way you will capture that moment in time. By recalling the details that delighted you, you will be more able to communicate those details and express the mood on your page. I have already talked about the images, memorabilia, and words you can include on a scrapbook page. Now, how do you put these elements together in a way that is pleasing to the eye? One of the main factors is composition.

Composition is defined as the way the components (shapes, lines, and colors) are arranged on the page. Where and how you decide to place these

items on the page results in the *layout*. In scrapbooking, the components are photos, memorabilia, words, die cuts, stickers, ink designs, and so forth.

Guidelines for Composition

Good composition brings relationship and harmony to the various elements used. This simply means that the pieces should work well together on the page and should be visually connected in some way. You can accomplish this by using shapes and sizes that complement each other. Then, create visual interest by using a variety of these shapes and sizes for contrast. Successful pages, whether simple or complex, make use of both consistency and contrast.

This page shows simply how consistency and contrast work. You can see *consistency* in the use of all basic geometric shapes that are similarly cut (all with smooth edges). *Contrast* is brought in by the cropping of one into a small circle and by the combination of close-up shots with faraway ones. The result is that you notice and enjoy each photograph more than if they were all taken from the same distance. The variety also gives you a feel for the overall scene—close-up shots that reflect Cade's expressions of pleasure and discovery and landscape shots that indicate the atmosphere in which he was toddling around.

Also notice that the small picture on the page functions as the focal point. Why is this? There are two reasons: first, it is the photo of greatest difference (con-

This simple layout has consistency and contrast.

trast) in size, and second, it is the only place where the photos overlap. Notice how I placed the picture at the intersection of four white areas. The result is that these white areas, negative spaces, work like arrows that direct your eye. *Negative space* is the shape of the empty spaces created when the objects are arranged on the page. They can often be a useful part of a composition. There was just enough variety and color within this group of pictures that other elements (die cuts, stickers, and so on) were not needed.

The page below was inspired by the words on a personalized lullaby tape we ordered from Cheshire Recordings. The words in "Rollin' and a-Strollin'" were the perfect accompaniment to the bottom photo, which shows Jenna and Lia taking Cade for a ride in their dolly stroller. I chose the other three photos to support the lyrics that led to the last picture.

The page is another illustration of how good composition works. Notice what provides consistency and contrast on this simple page and ties together the random photographs. The four bold blocks of primary colors and the treatment of a caption cutout in each provide consistency. Each photo also overlaps onto the plain background, bringing a flow of movement to the page and making the background a connected part of the design. The variety of colors and shapes of the solid blocks provide contrast. The simple hand-cut visuals, a moon and a sun, bring at once consistency and contrast. They are both heavenly bodies; but one is soft and smooth, the other bright and sharp.

I treated each picture on this page consistently by extending it over the mat and onto the background.

Repeated
shapes (on
this page,
arches) create
consistency.

Now look at this example of composition (at left). Again, notice the consistency and contrast. The shapes of the three large elements and the photographs within them create consistency—all six are cut in an arched shape (the bowl, an inverted one). The repetition of design, with gingerbread boys at the top and bottom of the page and the bowl cut out of red paper to pick up the color of Jenna's shirt, contributes to the consistency. Using the light-colored bags against the darker bowl and die cut helped achieve contrast. I created size contrast for the larger elements by using the smaller die cut, wooden spoon handle, and stickers. Notice how the pieces overlap one another, tying together the page.

Another way to lay out a balanced page is to repeat less obvious shapes on the page. Notice the repeated triangle formations in "Tea for Two" (opposite) that contribute to consistency even though the pictures were cut quite differently. You can see triangles in the napkin at the top, in each of the teacup images at the top, in the rectangle-circle combination matted in pink, in the three silhouetted images, and alone in the bottom middle image.

Also providing consistency are the use of pink throughout the page, the repeated scalloped motif, and the dots.

The goal of composition is to draw your eye first to the most important element or photograph, then around the page (enjoying each aspect), and finally back to the main element. This main element is called the *focal point*.

As you begin your page, consider which item is the most important, and then lay out the page with that piece as the focal point. If all the pictures you are using on this page are the same size, how do you make one more prominent? An easy way is by matting that picture more boldly than the others on the page. *Matting* is placing a photograph on a wider piece of paper that functions as a frame. Cut a wider mat for this picture, double-mat it and single-mat the rest, or add an extra color or design element around that one picture to get it the attention you desire.

You can place a focal point anywhere, although usually the item of greatest weight (or size) looks better in the central or lower third of the page. When combining the focal point with the other items, you want to bring balance to the page.

The easiest way to envision this concept is to think of a seesaw. You want to counter a large element with several smaller ones (or a grouping) that are comparable to the first in the amount of area covered or in intensity. Of course, there are countless ways to achieve this. Any sizable item on the page will be part of this balance, whether it is a photograph, paragraph of journaling, memorabilia, or a large decorative item (such as a die cut).

Repeating shapes can bring about good composition. Crop your photos, then place them on the page in a way that subtly duplicates a shape; in this case, triangles.

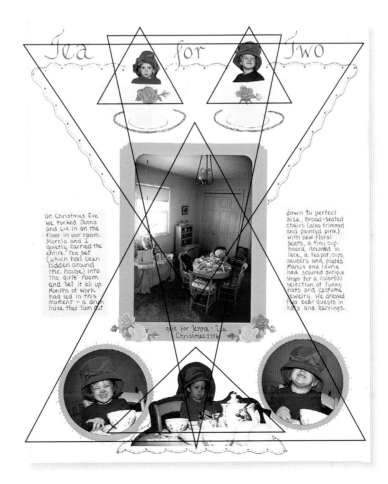

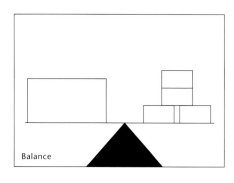

Balance

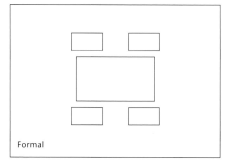

Formal

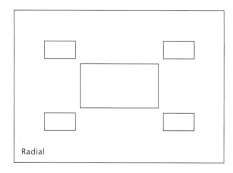

Radial

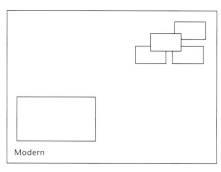

Modern

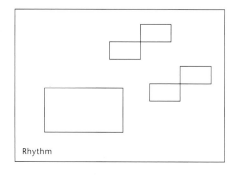

Rhythm

TYPES OF COMPOSITION

Formal or traditional composition is squared, even, and symmetrical.

Radial design places the main element at the center with supporting features arranged from the middle outward like a sunburst.

Informal or modern layout has a more uneven look but still maintains balance.

Rhythm (and movement) can be achieved by repeating a design in various places on the page. Overlap identical shapes or place prominent color at several areas around the layout.

MANY OR FEW PHOTOGRAPHS

I've used as many as eighteen photographs on a two-page spread and as few as three. A page full of pictures can be very effective when you place the photos in mini groupings on the page or have a definite progression. Using fewer photos allows you to emphasize the written or decorative elements of the story.

The two-page spread on page 61 shows how you can compose a layout with many pictures. These pictures are all quite similar in content, but you can achieve the same results with more varied photos. Here you see consistency in the checked matting paper and cutout letters that match Cade's checked pants. Placing the smaller pictures (mostly circles and ovals) in groupings brings more order to the page. I brought in contrast by the use of large rectangle shapes with the smaller circles (a size *and* shape difference). Matting the one picture in turquoise gives it contrast from the others and emphasizes its relationship to the card. The color combination of black and white always provides a strong element of contrast.

Tying Elements on Your Page Together

Use background paper and/or accent colors that pull out the most important features in the photographs and work with the whole group of photos.

Mat all the photos on the page in the same combination of colors.

Overlap some of the elements on the page.

Use small strips or geometric shapes of colored paper to support and accent the photos and bring balance to the page.

Sometimes I put together a page that is well balanced and has good color choices but still seems to be lacking something. The pieces need a little something more to be tied together well. Use some finishing touches to achieve this.

- Make a paper or ink border around the outside edge of the entire page.
- Use similar ink or sticker treatments around all the elements.
- Use small decorative accents (small stickers or ink designs) to overlap onto the background or another mat or between the photographs to draw your eye from one area of the page to the next. This prevents the pieces from floating alone on the page.

Placing photos in clusters can create a well-organized layout.

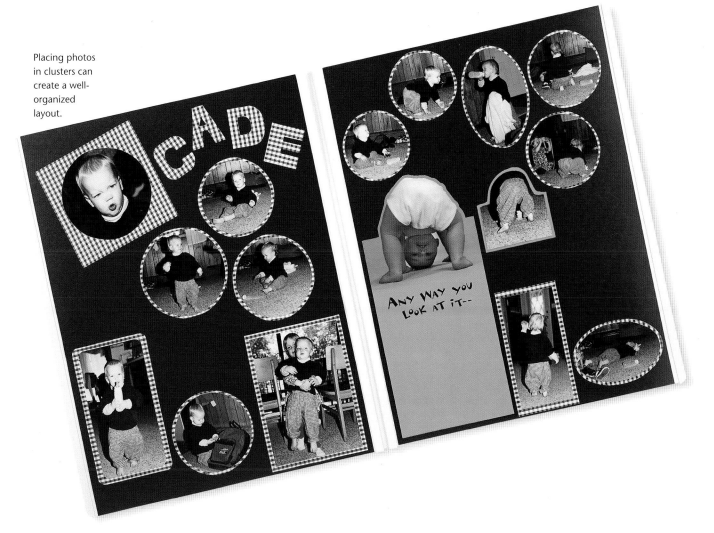

Building a Page

Many beginning scrapbookers are puzzled when faced with the decisions involved in putting together their pages. The following steps will help you successfully complete almost any page regardless of theme.

1. Select the photographs and any memorabilia you would like to use in one page's layout.
2. Determine the general idea, theme, or mood of the page. Consider the elements you may be able to use to enhance the layout.
3. Choose paper colors that complement the photos and fit the mood of the event. Try your photos against several choices to see what colors bring out the images best. Decide which two to four colors will look best.
4. Select a variety of die cuts and stickers that work with your theme.
5. Consider the amount of space you will need for journaling. Write a rough draft if you want.
6. Consider cropping your photos to keep all the important elements and contribute to the look of the layout.
7. Cut (trim, shape, or silhouette) the photos.
8. Decide which die cuts to use.
9. Lay out photos, memorabilia, die cuts, and any large accent pieces. (It may take some experimenting to balance your page well.)
10. Mat photos on colored paper. Mat memorabilia on buffered paper or enclose it in a photo-safe plastic envelope.
11. Recheck your layout for balance.
12. Mount photos, memorabilia, and die cuts on the page. If you are journaling on a die cut, do the writing first and then secure it to the page.
13. Add decorative stickers, pen designs, and captions.

Tips for Composition

An odd number of key elements creates more interest to the eye than does an even number. (A small grouping of pictures would count as a single element.)

Most pages look good if you cut the photographs in just a few similar shapes. Too much variety is less pleasing to look at.

Good composition requires a balance in busyness as well. It is a good idea to leave some blank space on the page. This doesn't mean gaping white holes, just some areas that don't present a lot of activity. Have you noticed that some highly decorated pages are hard to enjoy because there is so much vying for your attention? More is not always better!

For a lively looking album, vary your approach to composition throughout the album. This will help each page to be special and will make the scrapbook more enjoyable as a whole.

For heritage albums, use a similar layout throughout the book—it is often most attractive.

When using larger decorative items on the page, make a wider mat for the photos to keep them as the focal point.

Neatness will give your page its best look, so cut smoothly and mark lines on your pages lightly before journaling.

WORKSHOP: COMPOSITION

GOAL Achieve more variety in your layouts.

ASSIGNMENT Experiment with varying approaches for a group of photos and decorative elements

STEPS Select four to six photos that you would use in a single layout. (Since we are practicing here, be sure you have doubles or negatives of these photos.)

Crop the pictures however you prefer. (Do not mat them for this exercise.)

Choose some die cuts that would work with the theme.

Arrange the photos and die cuts in the following ways:

- Evenly spaced on the page (formal layout)
- Clustered in groups (informal layout)
- One piece in the center with others around it (radial layout)
- Overlapped a bit so each piece is connected to the others

You will see how trying a variety of approaches can help you find the best layout for any particular group of photos.

Color

Besides composition, color is the most important factor in achieving a good scrapbook page. It is a powerful resource. Consider the effect of walking into a room that is splashed with a variety of vivid hues playfully dancing together, though never moving. How different is your reaction when you enter a place draped in soft colors and are, without words, invited to rest. Each scrapbook layout will be a place where your reader will tarry for at least a few moments; some family members will accumulate hours poring over the pictures and stories you record. Your goal is to make each page a pleasing place to visit, inviting the reader in to receive what you've preserved for them.

More than with any other factor, you can set the tone for the entire page with the choice and combination of colors. Was the event a large gathering with much celebration or a quiet moment shared by just a few? Your color choices will do much to create the mood.

Choosing Good Colors for a Page

Most often you will select the decorative colors based on those in the photographs. Perhaps one decorative color will match a color in a photo exactly, or be its complement. Occasionally, you will choose colors in order to emphasize the holiday or season of the year (though they should never clash with those in the photos).

If your photo has a light edge, a dark mat is often most attractive. If the edge is dark, try a light-colored mat.

You will probably choose matting papers from colors within the photo.

If you are just beginning to work with color in regard to your photographs or would like to improve your skill, start by selecting solid colors to more clearly determine what best brings forth the most important aspect of each picture. This will help you to home in on the right basic colors, such as reds, blues, pinks, or greens. Once you determine the colors you will use, you can incorporate patterned papers of those colors into your layout.

Let's consider three examples of how good colors are chosen.

The paper used in the example at the top left perfectly matches the wooden flower in the photo. You can choose a color based on a single small element like this, but it must also work with the picture as a whole. The mustard color's warm tone is also similar to the deck's railing and slats and certainly emphasizes the lighter cast in Cade's fair skin and blond hair. Because the edge of the photo is primarily darker colors, this brighter paper surrounding it helps to bring out the lighter elements while enabling the viewer to appreciate the rich greens and blues.

The color of the mat can help pull out less prominent colors in the photograph.

There are multiple prominent colors in the photo at the top right. Placing it on pastel colored papers washed out the picture too much. This dark green worked well by supporting the background and foreground greens that surround Laurie and Alex and bring the focus onto them.

Again, with this picture (right), several colors could have worked well. I decided on this one because it was the least prominent of the colors in the gift wrapping and helped to draw it out. The bright pink was

a less desirable choice since Alex is a boy, and the yellow was so vivid that it brought more attention to itself than to the picture. The turquoise served to complement the warm tones of the cabinet and Alex's face.

Let me walk you through the color selection process for a photo.

I began by observing the various colors in this picture (right) and pulling sheets of six colors that matched those: turquoise and plum (from Lia's clothing), forest and kelly green (to pick up the shades in the grass and trees), and light and dark brown (colors similar to the fence and the foreground). In this instance, as with many pictures, any of these could have been fairly attractive, but there was, most likely, a color or combination that would be a step above the rest. That is the one I wanted to find.

I laid the photo on each sheet of paper. You will notice that although the darker shades (plum, forest green, and brown) match the photo, they don't enhance the look of it in any way. Since Lia is already framed in a large area of dark color, those colors blended too much with the edges of the photo itself. The turquoise and kelly green are a little too bright and pull your eye toward the paper rather than the picture. The light brown surprisingly (since it is not prominent in the photo) brings your attention to Lia's face. I realized when placing the picture on this color that it perfectly matched the color of her hair. It was also quite close to the color of the shadows at the top of her cheekbones. Your eye is now drawn right to her face; consequently, the color is a great choice for this picture.

You can incorporate color in your layout in several ways. You can use it as an overall background for the page, through smaller decorative additions (such as the use of die cuts, stickers, and memorabilia), as borders, or in ink accents you include. But perhaps the easiest way to begin bringing color to the page is by matting your pictures.

68 ....

LASTING MEMORIES

Matting

A *mat* is the paper attached directly beneath the photograph that extends around it to create a border. As cropping is the first frame of a photograph, matting provides the second frame. Matting is the way to begin establishing the color and defining the theme of the page. It is also the easiest way to set apart one photo as the focal point, by the emphasis created from a more noticeable mat. This is easy to do. Look at the following examples, created from only three different photographs.

The colors in these pictures (blue and red in Cade's outfit, green and brown in the background, and light tones in Cade's face and hair) offer us many options.

You can see how certain examples are more prominent than others. The width and combination of papers that make up the mat create very different effects. Some of the mats add just a bit of color so the photo will be framed on the page. Others communicate much more of a story and play a more decorative role. You can incorporate almost any of your scrapbooking materials with the mat; small

You can use matting in innumerable ways to emphasize the theme.

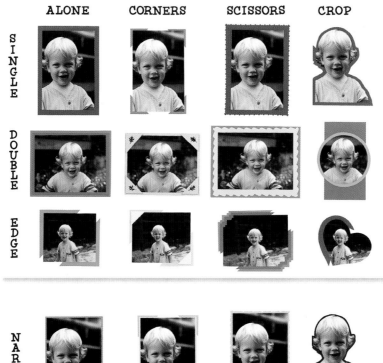

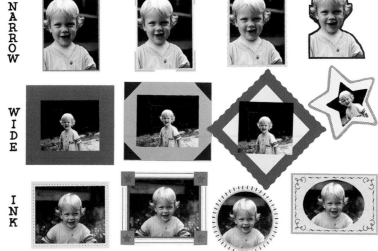

stickers, die cuts, and ink details are easy to use. Experimenting with variety here is great fun! Note that the matting treatments don't overpower the photos. You do, after all, want to keep the pictures as the focal point!

Note that close-up facial photos can be easily decorated; group photos (or any picture with smaller images) need to be matted more carefully so as not to overpower the picture.

Black-and-white photographs can work with any color of matting; in fact, most shots will look a little too bland if not mounted at all (especially ones from the 1950s that have a white border). I've had great success using bright shades and pastels. You can usually approach a layout using black-and-white photos the same way you would a similar color photo.

For older, sepia-toned photographs, most any color of brown will work as a mat. Using two shades of brown in a double mat is beautiful! Other combinations that will work well are any brown with black, brown or black with forest green, or black alone.

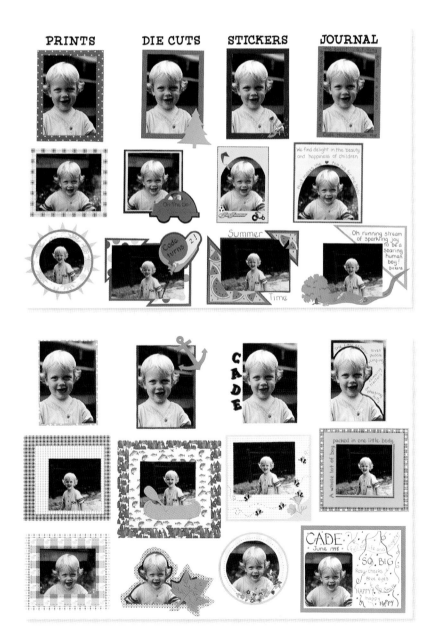

Consistency and contrast come into play regarding color selection, just as they did with composition. In most layouts, use colors that are either similar in intensity or varying values of one color. Either will provide consistency. Incorporating with them a neutral white, cream, or black (or other light or dark colors) can make a wonderful contrast.

You will want to have a basic idea of the overall plan for the page before you begin actually matting the pictures, since it is important that all the elements work well together. For an attractive page, approach the photographs first as a group. Randomly choosing various papers to mat the individual photos could cause you to end up with a very disjointed page. After your initial selection of colors, you will be able to work from there to create the right balance and specific paper for each picture.

Usually I start with a handful of photos that I want to use in one layout and select a variety of colors that I think may accent the pictures well. I always choose the colors before I begin to do any cropping, since my treatment of the picture may depend on what the color emphasizes in the photo. I spend a bit of time with this, as the color choices heavily impact the finished page.

After you choose several colors that seem to work well together, begin to narrow your selection by experimenting with the order in which you'll layer them under each of the photos. Sometimes the color you thought would be perfect as the mat will prove to be a better background, while your second color choice can be used as the mat. Often a photo will look wonderful if you double-mat it, using a third color choice for the page's background. (See Chapter 3, top of page 19.) It is important that you lay all of the pictures on the papers *before* beginning to mat any of them. Does your selection seem to work? This is the time to make changes until you are satisfied with the general color scheme.

Making a Page

Let me walk you through my entire process of color selection and distributing color on the page to create interest and balance.

Here is group of rather typical photos (below). How could I make them into a great page?

I began with the selection of paper colors. Each picture has a significant amount of neutral color: the dark house, the gray driveway, and the black bicycle.

I could have used grays and black, but they are here in such quantity that the page would probably be too drab if I did.

The more lively colors in these photos come from the children's clothing and the strips of green grass. Since the activity was playful, I used paper in those bright colors. I could also use black as a contrast to the colored papers and to emphasize the bicycle. I took care to use the vivid hues in carefully controlled amounts (such as very thin mat widths) so as not to overpower the photos.

It seems that these colors, above, work well. Next I began to experiment with how to best layer the colors for each photo and which color would provide the best background. Most seemed to look better when I placed the brighter color on black. I decided the close-up with Alex, Jenna, and Cade would probably work well when cut silhouette-style, as a point of interest on the page. I would decide whether to mat it depending on space.

Next I cropped the pictures to save space and to emphasize the best in them.

I determined to crop the pictures into a circle, an oval, and rectangles based on the elements I didn't want to eliminate— the background cars, hose, and cooler. Plus I wanted to stay with simple shapes. The silhouetted picture works well.

I had hoped to include a black bicycle die cut, but even after cropping, there wasn't enough room on the page. I silhouetted the last picture (at the bottom center of the page) on the top half, providing an emphasis of the bike that works much the way a die cut would have.

Before deciding the final arrangement of pictures on the page, I wrote out several sentences to journal right onto the page when the photos were finally in place. Once I arranged the pictures on the page, I adjusted the size of the matting paper slightly, cut it, and attached it. The page looks more balanced because I placed all but one of the photos against black paper. The silhouetted

BIKE
WASHING

When Alex began
washing his
bicycle, Jenna,
Lia and Cade
soon joined
in. They
were quite a
team! Every-   one took a little job and
no one doused anyone else with water — amazing!

sections stand out best unmatted. I carefully overlapped the pictures to tie the elements on the page together well.

The last step was writing the title, date, and sentences. The layout seemed to need just a bit of a final touch, remedied by careful use of dotted accents to add some detail without outlining everything. The splashes near the title give final definition to the page.

The Scrapbook of a World War II Navy Wave

There was energy in how she moved and how she spoke—a determined woman, I thought, and my first impression proved to be right on target. Her sense of adventure displayed itself quickly.

The spry, white-haired lady, Janet Keeler, introduced herself at the door and guided me to the well-lit kitchen table and then through the scrapbook that she had pulled off the closet shelf a few days before, for the first time in years. In the turning of the pages, her memories began to flow.

World War II was in progress. Janet Sturtevant was a twenty-year-old young woman from Nutley, New Jersey. She pointed out the U.S. Navy's promotional piece on a page in her album. "Wave job—to replace Navy men at shore stations," "$200 worth of clothes free!" And "Earn up to $126 monthly—plus allowances."

Janet said, "I had 60 percent of the guts to go into the service, and my friend Helen had 60 percent, so together we had more than enough!" The two young women with courage bolstered from each other's presence proceeded to the New York City recruiting station to volunteer for duty. The date was May 6, 1944. Paperwork was soon completed—the girls would leave in just three weeks. Send-off parties began with many friends and family clearly supporting the commitment Janet had made. (Apparently some of her mother's friends were appalled that she had enlisted.) Janet and I leafed through several more pages filled with the saved invitations, party favors, and heartfelt messages of good wishes. Some of the little cards were addressed to Short Wave Sturtevant, reflecting Janet's tiny stature!

Helen and Janet packed their bags and headed to Hunter College in Brooklyn, New York, for boot camp—six weeks of learning the rules of the navy, marching, cleaning the barracks, marching, learning the ship information, marching, learning the responsibilities of service, and marching. "We marched everywhere—even to lunch and dinner," Janet recalled.

Finally their initiation to navy life and its basic training were over. Janet and Helen graduated in a group of 3,500 on the second anniversary of the Waves, July 30, 1944. At the ceremony, the graduates passed in review before New York Mayor F. H. LaGuardia, who was seated in the VIP viewing area. Janet had passed the testing to admit her into a new position. She would soon master the necessary skills, and then this very petite woman was going to train the sailors to shoot anti-aircraft weapons!

The men came for two-week stretches and, under her direction, learned to assemble and disassemble twenty-millimeter, forty-millimeter, and fifty-caliber guns. She taught them how to lead a plane (aim ahead of it for accurate hitting) and how to compensate in aiming for the swelling of water as the ships moved over a bobbing sea. For three months she was stationed in Mississippi, and then she went on to another training site in San Diego to continue her job of equipping the men for the mission at hand.

San Diego was good to Janet. The work was rewarding, and it was there that she met a tall, handsome sailor also stationed on base. Walt Keeler was his name—the man who would become her husband after the war ended. They had shared a happy life for fifty years when Walt passed away in November of 1996. Janet's voice caught briefly with emotion as her thoughts and narrative returned to those days in San Diego. But she continued telling her story.

It was easy to detect the pride she felt at having served her country and her satisfaction in contributing to the war effort. Part of it was reflected in her album by the messages of encouragement she had received. Her scrapbook is sprinkled with wonderful greeting cards emblazoned with red, white, and blue. Being from another generation, I had not realized the magnitude of support expressed to those in the military during those years. Greeting card companies had designed messages for specific branches of service and had plentifully printed them to be purchased and sent around the world to encourage the troops. Janet had received numerous cards with messages like "To Our Favorite Wave!" I

was inspired! Her album catches the patriotic fervor and support of a country united with every intention of winning the battle.

This scrapbook, reflecting the same war my father and uncle had served in, is a window with a slightly different view of the war, yet it shows something of the common experience of those in military service. It also reveals the challenges for the loved ones who waited for their safe return home. The messages in Janet's album showed me the perspective of the friends and relatives whose loved ones were away in an uncertain war scenario.

As Janet was preparing to leave for that first stint in boot camp, another of her friends named Helen wrote these verses, "To a Girl in Navy Blue."

> I feel like crying
> But I'll try to be brave
> Because you're leaving
> To be a Wave.
>
> You're starting out
> On a life that's new
> And you can bet
> I'm going to miss you
>   (An awful lot.)

We certainly had fun
These past two years
With our corny wisecracks
Puns, jokes and jeers.

Please drop us a line
When you have time—
If not a letter
Then, just a short rhyme.

Even a card or a note
Will do—
As long as we know
Where they've sent you.

So 'bye, Jan, for now—
And GOOD LUCK to you,
In every single
Thing that you do.

We'll be thinking of you
And waiting for
That First Furlough!

The words Janet spoke were to me, but her thoughts were clearly far away. She said, "I know it was war, but I have good memories—really good memories of that time." I'm so glad she has her marvelous scrapbook to help bring them back.

More Examples of Good Color

Here, on the "Happy Easter!" spread on page 76, the outfit Cade was wearing determined my color selection. The blue, plum, and cream were easy to transfer into designs on the eggs, and I duplicated the striped pattern to further tie the photos and eggs together. Since purple and yellow are colors often associated with Easter (and are complementary colors as well), using the bright yellow daffodil stickers made a good accent. You can incorporate brighter accent colors, as I did here, just do so in smaller amounts than the main colors.

My friend Beth made this "Who Loves Gracie?" page (see page 77), keeping the background fairly simple to compensate for the many silhouetted photos she wanted to use in the layout. Her color choice offers some brightness without overpowering the photos, and because the colors have similar intensity, they offer consistency. She easily positioned the random photos, with their many color variations, on the color that worked best for each. She cut the background blocks into slightly different sizes, bringing a subtle contrast and interest. She also achieved contrast by setting the busy shapes on a very plain background.

Varying tones of one color can create a very nice looking page. On the Grace Elizabeth Feia page (see page 77), Beth used several shades of purple to bring in contrast and consistency. (Remember the paint swatch card example?) Notice how

I chose these colors specifically to match those in Cade's outfit, with the bright yellows added as an accent.

she used a solid, strong color to mat the pictures and then placed them on lighter and lighter solids and prints as she continued working to the base of the page.

This pumpkin scene (see page 78) incorporates patterned paper with the solids. The touches of patterned paper, grouped in bunches, bring a little flair and interest that fit the theme and introduce a manageable bit of the stronger burnt orange as an accent.

You can see how well the matting paper works with the colors in the picture. A more typical bright pumpkin orange would have been too strong and made the pictures look washed out. The less-used brown and black mats serve to bring variety to the page.

Primarily using patterned papers in a layout can work well. The U.S. flag theme (on page 78) was a given, with Cade playing in the patriotic bandanna we had tied on his head. Since the striped background is very bold, a darker, contrasting blue print was a good choice for the mat, as it worked to break up the flow of red and white. The white dots in the mats have a look similar to the stars on a field of blue that I used on the cutout flag; thus I could use a different paper without it looking like there are too many things going on. This page's fun hand-cut visual is the primary focus, but the photos are still easily noticed. Notice that the deep red paper used for the flag stripes is a shade darker than the cherry red in the background paper. Using the deep red gives the page a more three-dimensional look.

Combining solid colors makes a simple yet interesting background that looks great with silhouettes.

Using varying shades of one color can make a beautiful page.

Add accents
with printed
papers to
emphasize
your theme.

Contrasting
papers let mul-
tiple prints work
successfully.

HOW TO CREATE GOOD COLOR COMBINATIONS

Remember the principles of the color wheel. You may want to purchase one to help guide you as you work. Good color combinations are typically achieved in the following intervals:

- **Complementary**—Directly opposite on the color wheel
- **Related**—Beside each other on the color wheel
- **Triad**—Three colors that are an equal distance apart
- **Split-complementary**—Using three colors, one of your choosing and the other two being situated on either side of its complement
- **Achromatic**—A combination of black, white, and grays
- **Monochromatic**—Varying shades of one color

Here are some other successful color combinations:

- A selection of clear, bright tones
- Crisp fall colors
- Fresh spring hues
- Delicate pastels
- Soft, muted shades

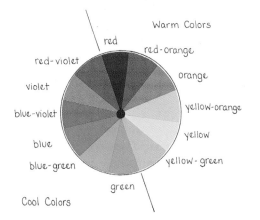

Familiarizing yourself with the rules of the color wheel will help you in selecting good color combinations. .

Use a combination of colors with similar intensity. Then add a light or dark color for contrast.

8

Materials You Will Use in Making Your Scrapbook

As you create a scrapbook page, you will use several materials to make it attractive and symbolize the story: solid and patterned papers, pens, die cuts, and stickers. The possibilities for using and combining these are endless. In this chapter I will suggest various ways you can make use of them. Expanding your approach in this will help you to create unique pages that truly capture the occasion.

Paper

Paper is the most foundational decorative material used in a scrapbook. Its color immediately sets the tone for the entire page. You can use it as the full background, as a mat for the photographs, in die cuts, or to create decorative pieces limited only by your imagination. There are dozens of shades to choose from and a variety of weights as well.

Card stock is a heavier-weight paper that you can cut with precision to achieve a clean, definite edge. Using it will help you avoid the wrinkling and tearing that sometimes result when using a lighter-weight paper. Card stock comes in solid colors. (Patterned papers are printed on lighter-weight paper.)

A babe in a house
is a wellspring of pleasure.

These two scrapbook pages show how you can use hand-cut decorations on your page. Of course, there are unlimited ways to do this.

Paper offers many options because of its versatility. Keep in mind the variety of ways you can use it:

Cut into any shape you choose (use an individual piece or a combination of shapes)

Torn to create softened edges

Folded to give a multidimensional look even though flat

Woven for a basket or checkerboard design

Layered (overlapping the colors) for visual depth (see Bahamas layout on page 83)

Stamped with images suiting your theme

Embossed for a formal look

Written on for interesting journaling

Pieced to create a mosaic, stained-glass, or puzzle-like visual

In thin strips to bring color balance to the page (see "Kyle" on page 85)

Tear the edges of your paper for a softer, irregular look.

Add thin strips of paper to your layout to quickly bring a balance of color to an otherwise finished page.

PATTERNED PAPERS

Patterned papers offer a quick decorative solution. Using them can immediately set the tone for your page by providing a look that can be bold and festive or soft and delicate. There are hundreds of wonderful patterns to choose from. But because of their design, you need to take a little more care when using them.

The challenge is often that the subjects in many photographs are rather small. Hence, a fairly bold pattern can easily overpower the photo, causing the images to become less of a focal point than you desire. One way to work with the patterned paper is to use it as the overall background and then mat the photograph on a coordinating solid color.

You can achieve the same effect when you double-mat the photo using a solid color first and then a second mat of patterned paper behind the solid. This creates a break between the patterned paper and the photo, bringing the focus back to the pictures while allowing the design of the paper to enhance the photo or define the event. Smaller patterns are easier to incorporate than larger ones and can quickly bring some excitement to many pages.

Here are some other ways to bring these versatile papers into your layout:

Use a small pattern as the mat for a picture.

Use a template to create a decorative piece to use as you would a die cut.

Use it to embellish a solid-paper die cut.

Cut or punch small shapes from it to use as small accents.

The kids asked to take their evening bath up at Jacob's. Beth kindly let them join him, gave them bubbly hair-dos and snacks!

Jenna, Lia and Jacob get fancy hair-dos.

Bath time at Grandma Betty's was always in the basement washtub when the kids spent the night. She could scrub them and wash their hair while standing. After the bath, they put on Grandpa Don's undershirts to sleep in.

May 1997

Small patterns (as in the polka-dotted paper here) work well as a mat.

Make small triangles to use as corners on or beneath the edge of a photo. You can embellish them with a punched shape, a sticker, or ink.

Cut it into squares and add an alphabet letter sticker on each to create a title for your page. Layer it with a solid also if you wish.

Use a narrow leaf stencil to make a ribbon border. You can further decorate these by adding tiny stickers or punched shapes to emphasize the theme. (See bottom right corner of "Merry Christmas" idea board on page 110.)

Cut it into letter shapes for a title.

Use a wide stripe pattern to create a picket fence. (Add plain white paper to make the horizontal pieces.) Then decorate the fence if you wish (see the "Stickers" idea board, page 90).

Keep your photos the focal point when using larger patterns of paper by matting the photos first in solids or small patterns.

CORN

JULY 1998

Alex · Jenna · Lia · Cade

The kids love getting corn from Sandy Hill Fruit Farm or a roadside stand. They pitch in to clean off the husks and silk. This scene was repeated often this year in the late summer.

Use a pattern that closely matches the fabric of clothes worn by someone in the photo to quickly bring the color scheme to a page.

Here are two tips for using larger patterns:

Cut it into strips to place around a photograph or evenly across the page to invite just a bit of the design onto the page.

Cut out part of the design to add as an accent.

Pens and Inks

Your pens are obviously used for journaling and writing captions. But they can provide you with the means for making other accents on your page. Perhaps you've just completed a layout, but the page seems to be lacking something. Often a few finishing touches can pull together the existing elements of the design to produce a better result. Use your pens to provide many of these tiny details or to embellish die cuts, stickers, or template designs in the following ways:

You can create borders for any theme in endless combinations with paper, ink, stickers, die cuts, and your tools.

Tiny ones to create a corner border

You can also embellish die cuts.

Draw accents on them with your pens.

Draw around them once they are on the page.

Add pieces of solid or patterned decorative paper to jazz them up.

Stickers

Stickers are plentiful in the scrapbooking world, having been made to suit almost any theme. They come in a variety of styles as well, to capture the objects in the style you need. Some are bright, primary colors; others are subdued pastels that fit with an old-fashioned or formal page. Normally it looks best when you use one company's stickers per page, since each manufacturer has a style of its own.

Stickers offer great versatility in scrapbooking.

Use a pattern that closely matches the fabric of clothes worn by someone in the photo to quickly bring the color scheme to a page.

Here are two tips for using larger patterns:

Cut it into strips to place around a photograph or evenly across the page to invite just a bit of the design onto the page.

Cut out part of the design to add as an accent.

Pens and Inks

Your pens are obviously used for journaling and writing captions. But they can provide you with the means for making other accents on your page. Perhaps you've just completed a layout, but the page seems to be lacking something. Often a few finishing touches can pull together the existing elements of the design to produce a better result. Use your pens to provide many of these tiny details or to embellish die cuts, stickers, or template designs in the following ways:

You can create borders for any theme in endless combinations with paper, ink, stickers, die cuts, and your tools.

One or more stripes around each photo or at the page's edge

Row of dots

Tiny squiggles

Basic geometric shapes

Simple holiday shapes or theme motifs, such as leaves, holly, flowers, snowflakes, pumpkins, pine boughs, or hearts, alone or combined with the other basic designs.

TIPS

Work carefully when using a new type of pen or paper. Avoid smudges by being aware that papers will absorb ink differently, and have varying drying times.

If you draw pencil lines to journal on, use a white art eraser to remove them and a soft three-inch-wide pastry brush to clear away the erasure shavings. This will prevent accidental wrinkling and tearing of photos, accent papers, or stickers.

Be on the lookout for easy border designs in magazines and advertisements. Save the sample or keep a sketch pad handy to jot down designs you can use later.

Cartoon Accents

Often a little cartoon accent (like those seen in comic strips) that expresses an action or emotion can bring definition or humor to your page. You can place these easy additions beside a photo or sticker to add a bit of the story to the visuals.

Place cartoon additions near your photos to emphasize the activity.

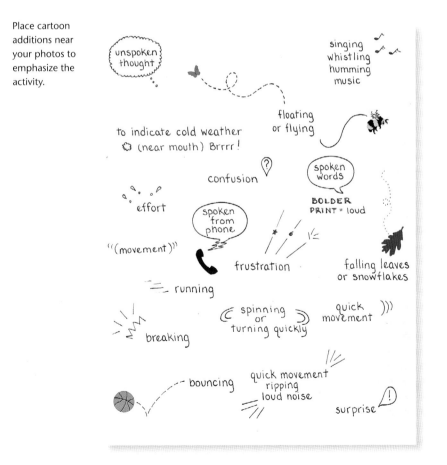

Die Cuts

Die cuts are precut paper shapes used as decorative accents on your pages. They come in a wide variety of shapes and colors to suit almost any theme. You can use them in several ways:

A single die cut as a bold accent

Several die cuts in a grouping to create a border or a scene

Journaled on as a title or in telling the details of the story

As a mat for a small photograph

Cut in half, using one or both pieces at the sides of the page

Die cuts come in hundreds of shapes to support almost any theme.

Try various ways of incorporating die cuts into your layouts.

Tiny ones to create a corner border

You can also embellish die cuts.

Draw accents on them with your pens.

Draw around them once they are on the page.

Add pieces of solid or patterned decorative paper to jazz them up.

Stickers

Stickers are plentiful in the scrapbooking world, having been made to suit almost any theme. They come in a variety of styles as well, to capture the objects in the style you need. Some are bright, primary colors; others are subdued pastels that fit with an old-fashioned or formal page. Normally it looks best when you use one company's stickers per page, since each manufacturer has a style of its own.

Stickers offer great versatility in scrapbooking.

A time line can represent a large span of time in a little space.

You can use stickers in a number of ways:

Individually, they are tiny accents or can note the beginning or end of a caption.

In a grouping, they can define the theme, create a pictorial scene, or make a border.

In large numbers, they become a wonderful floral bouquet or a filled toy box.

As I was brainstorming for the pages I would make for Jacie's graduation album, I looked through her other scrapbooks and calendars, writing a list to be sure I didn't miss any important activities. About three-quarters of the way through I realized that I had stickers representing most of them. The time line I created using the stickers was an easy way to document the milestone moments in eighteen years of growth.

Tools You Will Use in Making Your Scrapbook

*S*crapbookers now have the luxury of a wonderful variety of tools made for their use. The many options offer you endless possibilities in creatively preserving your memories. I will describe the basic tools and how you can use them in this chapter, but you may have tools from other crafts that you could adapt for use in your scrapbooking as well.

Templates

You can use templates as a pattern for cutting a photograph or piece of paper into a shape. *Templates* are shapes cut into a sheet of plastic in various sizes of one shape (circles or ovals) or a variety of shapes (different flowers). Some templates are cut with several shapes to support a theme (birthday, baby, vacation, or holiday).

You can use templates in several ways:

Draw the shape onto the photograph and then cut it out.

Draw the shape onto a piece of decorative paper to cut out and use as an accent or mat.

Draw the shape directly onto the page to journal in or embellish.

Using the template as a stencil, fill in the design with a pen or sponge some ink right into the shape with a make-up sponge and a pigment ink pad.

Star shapes in various sizes were used in this two-page spread.

STENCILS

Stencils are similar to templates but usually have more detail. Lettering stencils have become very popular with scrapbookers. There are hundreds of other stencils that you can use, and their themes and styles cover the gamut. Use them with pens, paper paint, or ink (as described in "Templates" on page 93), or use the stencil as a basic pattern, drawing the design onto paper and cutting it out to incorporate into your layout.

BORDER TEMPLATES

Border templates come on a long strip of plastic (or at the edge of some shape templates) and provide a pattern for making a decorative border around your pictures or the entire page. They are available in a variety of styles: Victorian, zigzag, waves, and so on. You can use border templates with ink or to create a design you cut from paper.

Use a decorative template and a pen to make a frame for the entire page.

Cut a border from decorative paper in the width of your choice, and then use adhesive to secure the paper to your page.

Cut a decorative mat.

Add stickers, die cuts, or snippets (see "Snippets" on page 98) to any of the above ideas, and then thread them together with ink dots or lines.

Draw full-sized borders or small accent lines anywhere on your page.

Border templates can add interest to a relatively full page.

Use different types of pens to vary the border design: bold-tip pens create wide lines, calligraphy pens give a formal look, and fine-point pens can make narrow lines, dots, and other small details.

Draw a single wavy line, shift the template and redraw the line, and then fill in your lines for a beautiful ribbonlike border.

SIMPLE SHAPES DO IT!

You can use the templates (or other small shapes cut by hand) to make basic geometric shapes that are easy to work with and represent a multitude of objects. You can use them in many ways in your layouts. Start with the basic shape, and then decorate it to be anything you wish.

Here are some ideas:

Circles: balls, coins, doughnuts, life rings, wheels, wreaths, ornaments, simple flowers, globe, beads, marbles, checkers, buttons, plates, eyes or glasses, bubbles, hula hoops, balloons, cookies, clocks, sun, steering wheel, compass, bugs, peppermint candy, jingle bells, full moon, berries, grapes, cherries, oranges, 78- or 45-rpm records (Remember those?)

Ovals: frames, eggs, simple flowers, football, eyes or glasses, beads

Squares: blocks, frames, houses, presents, dice, quilt parts, windows, books

Rectangles: frames, doors, train cars, candles, books, presents, playing cards, buildings, windows, pillows, envelopes, flags

Combine simple geometric shapes to create interesting visuals for your page.

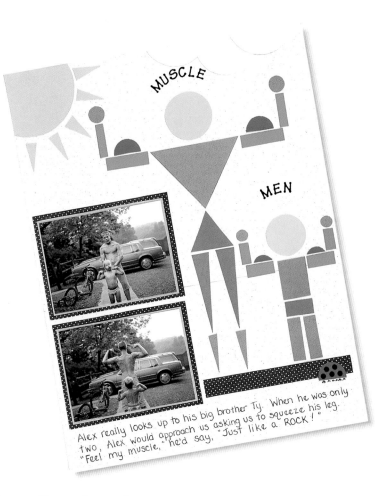

Alex really looks up to his big brother Ty. When he was only two, Alex would approach us asking us to squeeze his leg. "Feel my muscle," he'd say, "Just like a ROCK!"

Triangles: *trees, sailboats, flags and pennants, ice cream cones, roofs, kerchiefs, mountains, angel's body or wings, clown hats, pieces of pie or cake*

Stars: *snowflakes, ornaments, magic wand, cookies*

Diamonds: *leaf, kites*

Hearts: *valentines, cookies, apples (if points are rounded a bit), butterflies (if pairs are positioned sideways with points together)*

Drops: *tears, rain, splashes, seeds, candle flame*

You can use simple combinations of these shapes to create many more objects, like snowmen, houses, crayons, and so forth.

Circle and Oval Cutters

Circle and oval cutters provide a wonderful shortcut for scrapbookers. They are adjustable tools, allowing you to cut either of these smooth shapes, in a wide range of sizes, in just seconds. These tools usually work most successfully with a photograph or card-stock-weight paper; lighter-weight papers tend to tear at the edges when you cut them with a circle or oval cutter. Replacing the blade as needed will help you to consistently cut a smooth edge.

Decorative Scissors

You have at your fingertips dozens of edges waiting to be used in your layouts. Decorative scissors for making special edges are readily available in scrapbooking or craft stores. You can quickly give your papers a little flair using these handy tools.

Here are some ways to use decorative scissors:

Cut the perimeter of a photo or mat or both.

Center the curve of a scalloped-edge scissor or other curved design at the corner of your photo for an easy variation of a rounded corner.

Cut both sides of a strip of solid or patterned paper to use as a border.

Cut accent pieces for your page like letters or geometric shapes.

Cut a piece to use like a die cut for decoration, or to journal on.

Cut a strip on one side of the paper with decorative scissors, the other side with straight scissors.

Accent your special edge using tiny punches to create a lacy border.

Create accents that the design specifically lends itself to—waves or clouds, for example.

But keep in mind that these scissors provide a lot of design in a small space. Use them carefully so as not to distract from your photographs. It is possible to use multiple scissors edges on a single layout, but here again, proceed with care and choose edges with similar designs. When cutting a photograph with a decorative edge, leave a bit more of the photo than you would otherwise. It will usually give the picture a better-sized first frame.

TIPS

Carefully line up the blade to match the design of your previous cut to create a smooth flow in the design.

When making a circle or oval in a paper or picture, cut from the bottom center spot. If the repeat of the design doesn't come out even, it will be less noticeable there.

If your scissors' blades dull over time, cut through a piece of aluminum foil to get them sharp again.

Alter or combine punched shapes to create even more options.

punch a strawberry

cut out a "w"

use as an ivy leaf

Paper Punches

Decorative paper punches are now available in a vast array of shapes and sizes.

You can use either the positive image *(the shape itself) or the* negative image *(the hole left from punching the shape).*

Use them individually as little accents or grouped together to create a border (for a photo or the page), a bouquet, or a scene.

Use patterned paper for an even greater variety.

Use scraps of cropped photos from your layout to create punched accents that will match the page perfectly.

Use a few punched shapes combined with some pen accents to add a finishing touch to your page.

Punch four small designs and place each in the center of a square or triangle cut from a paper that coordinates with your page. Use them at the corners of a photo or a mat.

Snippets

At the end of a scrapbooking session, take a few minutes before cleaning up and invest some time in using your small scraps of paper to create snippets. *Snippets* are small paper shapes used as accents on your pages. Even one square inch of paper (that you may have been inclined to throw away) is enough to make a snippet. I never use large scraps for them since they have many better uses.

From your punch inventory, choose punch designs that are most appropriate for the paper colors you've just used. Punch as many shapes as possible from each scrap and store all the colors of one shape in a small container or bag. Soon you will have a collection of

- Mini stars in shades of yellow or patriotic red, white, and blue
- Apples in autumn red, gold, and green
- Hearts in hues of pink, red, white, cream, and berry
- Flowers in any color you choose

You can hand-cut snippets in other shapes from small scraps of solid or patterned paper.

Craft Knives

Use a craft knife to produce tiny cuts for accents from your solid card-stock-weight paper. Use it to produce beautiful, intricate borders or cutouts that are especially nice in baby, heritage, or wedding albums.

This is a time-consuming touch but occasionally worth the effort for a special page.

TIPS

Cut your design from the middle outward, cutting the largest holes first and smallest ones last.

Trim the outside border as your final step.

For easiest cutting, work on a piece of glass or a self-healing mat (available at art supply stores).

Flexible Curves

A flexible curve is a wonderful scrapbooking tool. It is available in art supply stores and large office supply stores, located with the drafting supplies. You can maneuver a flexible curve to create just the curve you need. The material is flexible yet firm, so it will hold shape, enabling you to repeat the exact line in another place on your layout. Use a flexible curve for making lines to represent roads, vines, or hill slopes, or simply to caption or journal on.

Use a flexible curve to form just the shape you desire.

Rubber Stamps

The rubber stamp industry has boomed in recent years, making a multitude of options for your scrapbook. Beautiful, cute, and quirky stamps are abundant. Use them with pigment ink.

Use colored pencils to fill in the open areas of the stamped design.

Use a rubber stamp to print a design on a piece of paper; then cut it out, and add it to your page.

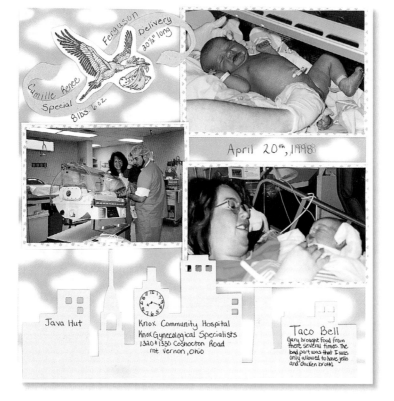

I used old metal typesetting dingbats to create the design on this heritage page.

In antique shops, I have purchased old typesetting metal stamps known as *dingbats*. They typically have delicate designs and work beautifully for accent touches in heritage albums.

You can use stamps to create an entire border for an individual photo or a whole page. To ensure a straight, even border, set the edge of the stamp along a deep-sided straightedge or a special tool made for this use.

Use stamps to create accents or an overall background design by evenly repeating the imprint on an entire page.

New Tools

Before purchasing a new tool, try to see it demonstrated at a craft or scrapbooking store. Attend a class on using it if possible. To discover any important details about its function, practice using the tool on scraps before working with your actual layout pieces. I have read numerous product reviews on scrapbooking tools, and it is clear that scrapbookers' preferences vary. One may love a certain tool, but using it may be awkward for someone else. If you can try it and are satisfied with its performance, or if a salesperson can show you some tricks in using it, you will be happy knowing you have purchased a product you like and can successfully use.

Let's Get Creative

Creative was not a word I had particularly associated with Debby. Granted, her home has always been very nicely decorated and is consistently neat as a pin. It's just that I'd never known of her being involved in a specific art expression or craft—until she began scrapbooking.

Well, Debby has been a delight to watch. As it turns out, she has a great eye for color *and* composition and has in the past year completed a vacation album, her wedding album, and a special ABC album commemorating dozens of loving gestures from a dear neighbor couple who were consistently there for her through some difficult years.

Debby is a wonderful example for other scrapbookers. Each of her albums has a different tone and is uniquely delightful. She successfully takes ideas, gives them a new twist, and makes them her own. Looking thoughtfully at her photographs, she determines what will accentuate them to achieve the look she wants. Then she dives in, adding little touches to create yet another marvelous page.

I appreciate the commitment I see in many scrapbookers. Mary Lou has made it a priority to complete albums for each of her four children. She continues to try new ideas from various sources to keep the project fresh and has produced hundreds of nice pages in less than two years.

As my own scrapbooking progressed and I increased my supply of tools and materials, I tried to convince my husband that the investment in the

The dress up box provides fun for hours.

Lia and Jenna
November 1999

They often proceed to a tea party with milk and cookies.

creative supplies was well worth the money I spent. "It's cheaper than therapy!" I told him. (Actually, scrapbooking can be therapeutic!) And I emphasized, "It's the only thing in my life that stays done!" With a large brood, the cooking, cleaning, and laundry are never caught up for long, so there is clearly something very satisfying about the scrapbooking process. And indeed, the creative expression can be one of its most enjoyable aspects.

I've walked you through the basic steps of scrapbooking and introduced some of the available tools and materials. Now it's time to let the fun take over! How can you help your creativity to flow? Later in this chapter there are several sections that will help you consider how to tell your stories creatively. But first, let me share some examples with you.

My friend Suzy is a master at creative expression. She is very artistic, but it is the other ways she approaches scrapbooking that continually impress me: the ways she uses available resources to create her pages. These are ideas that anyone could easily apply. Suzy has access to a good color copy machine, which she used in unusual ways to capture images for her layouts. She copied her favorite fabric prints, making her own background paper. She has photocopied antique baby

Photocopy special garments to work into your pages.

Elaborate pages can be well worth the extra effort (bottom left). A photocopy enlargement of the antique postcard provided the accent violets (bottom right).

Home Sweet Home ♡
This is our first house on Berkshire Dr.
Ypsilanti, Michigan. 1990-1998

Here Jacob learns to climb, swing & slide.

Neighbors & Friends
Thorntons, Chesters, Quinteros, Parris...

Oakwood Park across the street from our home.

We moved to Ohio in November 1998

Great layouts
can also be easy
and quick.

dresses, strips of lace and ribbon, and tiny patterned socks. (The reducing and repeat features on the machine turned the images into great borders.) She has also duplicated the front covers of favorite storybooks of her daughter, Charlie Beth, so she can incorporate them on album pages to evoke the memories of snuggly story times. The tiny reduced covers (approximately one and a half inches) make a delightful border.

Suzy photocopied her daughter's snowsuit and used the hood portion as part of the background paper for photos of the baby's first snow experience. Of course, it blends perfectly with the pictures (see page 104, top).

A copy machine allowed for easy accents on the "Easter Sunday" page (see page 104). The vintage postcard was going to be a key element. For accents to use with it, Suzy enlarged the postcard's image on the copier and then cut the flowers out to use in the layout. She made a relatively simple page exquisite! (She hand-punched the pink mats to achieve a lacy look.)

This "Brookside Gardens" page (on page 104) is one of my favorites from Suzy's album. She saw a photograph of a wrought-iron gate in a Sotheby's garden statuary auction catalog. She enlarged the photograph and traced the pattern of the left side of the gate onto thin paper with a soft pencil. She then flipped it over so that the penciled surface was touching her album page and retraced the design through the thin paper to transfer the light pencil markings onto the page. (The pencil rubbed off onto the page.) Then she traced the design from the backside of the paper, giving her the mirror image of the design, and repeated the same steps to make the right side of the gate. Then she darkened the pencil design, now complete on the page, with a black pigment pen. Suzy created the connecting arch to incorporate the name of the gardens her family had visited and where they had taken these pictures. The final step was using colored pencils in several shades of green to softly fill in the spaces. Suzy made the pink frame around the photographs by photocopying a strip of embroidered ribbon her mother had given her. The page took several hours to execute from start to finish but was clearly worth the effort!

I love observing the varied expressions scrapbookers use to bring their own style to a page. But creativity doesn't have to be time-consuming. Another friend, Beth, makes choices that can be quickly applied and still result in delightful pages.

This playground spread (on page 105) is one of my all-time favorites! Beth came in to my workshop for just a brief part of one evening. She sat down and pulled out the photos of her adorable son, Jacob, frolicking on some brightly colored playground equipment. Quickly deciding that primary colors were the way to go, she matted the pictures on solid paper and then briefly considered what she could add to accent them well. She decided on polka dots—the perfect playful touch! They certainly suited the mood of the page and were just the right size to add interest without distracting too much from the photos. In a matter of forty-five minutes, Beth had finished the entire page. Her sister calls this "wonking out pages." In any case, great pages don't have to be complicated!

Introductory or Dedication Pages

A great place to let the creativity reign is on the very first page of the album. Use this space well. It is the place to set the tone for the whole album. Here you can capture the subject's personality and interests if the album is focused on one person.

Lia was born in the wee hours of the morning. The nighttime image seemed suitable to accompany the newborn photograph, and the shades of blue complemented the picture's yellow tone.

It's easy to make oversized shapes or letters like these that nearly fill the page.

If the album is to be a gift, write the *to* and *from* information on the introduction page along with the identification of the event (fortieth birthday, golden anniversary, child's birth, vacation), including the dates of the event or celebration.

The moon was a suitable way to symbolize Lia's nighttime birth.

Developing the Theme

If you get stuck for ideas when developing your theme, how can you get your creativity flowing?

The approach outlined below can help you do this. It can guide you through a brainstorming process, helping you to consider the details that can spur ideas for your page.

When you are beginning to consider how a page will come together, it is helpful to determine all the elements you could include. Sit down with a piece of scrap paper and try to re-create the activity in your mind. What were the memorable things about it? Besides the obvious, were there supportive dynamics that made the day special? The following is a list of ideas that will help jog your memory a bit for anything you can include. Sometimes the less obvious elements are the ones that really help make a great page!

1. Identify the event or situation with the key pieces of information. Who? What? When? Where? Why?

2. List the highlights of the event, including the ones captured in the photos and the ones you remember that were not photographed.

3. List sensory recollections from this event. What did you see, touch, hear, smell, or taste? What added to the experience? Were there games, food, significant weather, or colors?

4. List objects associated with the event. What objects were actually there or are associated with this kind of event?

5. Then narrow down your elements. From the previous information, what do you want to record on this page that will represent the event the best and preserve the memory?

Begin to think about what aspects you might represent with paper, die cuts, stickers, and template shapes; then pull out anything you have in your supplies that might work with this page.

You may have to communicate some pieces of the story through the decorative elements or by writing a descriptive paragraph about the event. Here are some clever ways to get information on your page without recording it in the way you would typically journal or decorate.

Mount photos on plain or patterned paper that resembles clothing worn at the event (jeans and bandanas at a hayride, for example).

Lia received many adorable outfits as gifts when she was born. This border developed as a way to symbolize them without taking up much space on the heavily journaled page.

Float "aroma words" as captions or in the text.

Use words written in any color that matches your page to create borders around the photos or at the page's edge.

Include something funny that was (or could have been) said. Place the quote in a "balloon."

Try illustrating what the weather was like.

Use stickers and die cuts to help fill in details and illustrate what occurred.

If you don't have a photo, die cut, or sticker to represent a key part of the event, consider cutting the shape out of paper yourself. A child's picture dictionary can provide a great variety of simple shapes for this. Use one color, or several to make a more dimensional and detailed look.

Correspondence can be an important addition. Invitations, postcards, and notes can set the tone with style, color, and the handwriting of friends or family members.

Generating Ideas

How can you come up with good ideas? Usually I begin by thinking about a variety of visuals that could fit the theme on which I am working. For example, a birthday theme could revolve around gifts, balloons, streamers, cake, candles, or party hats. Then I move to this particular birthday—the guest of honor, his or her age, any special gifts or parts of the celebration. What unique aspects can I focus on that will capture it? How can I emphasize or illustrate them? Following this process of thinking can be quite helpful in moving you to the things that will best depict the event.

IDEA BOARDS

When I began teaching scrapbooking classes in my home, I made available to my students all the scrapbooks I had made, so they could browse through them for ideas. I also created idea boards for various themes. These are composed of dozens of combinations of decorative scrapbooking supplies. I wanted to help stretch my students' imaginations to come up with unique ways of using these examples in a layout, believing that they would find much satisfaction in the development of their own creative expressions. That was certainly the case—and they found it to be easy.

The boards became a key element of the workshops. New students were delighted to have an abundance of little ideas to adapt, and my longtime attendees often commented that they had just seen an idea that they never noticed before. The boards seemed to help them and expand their own confidence to be creative. It was working well. Then I taught them about translation.

TRANSLATION

Several years ago I realized I was surrounded by wonderful ideas in the graphics and color combinations in printed advertisements and magazine pages. I discovered I could easily adapt them to a scrapbook layout. I could *translate* the ideas I liked to fit the themes of my page.

Formal looks in elegant shapes are beautiful for heritage albums.

Represent winter holidays and activities with stickers and die cuts.

110 ....

LASTING MEMORIES

Capture the focus of almost any trip with die cuts and stickers that cover the gamut.

Emphasize your family celebrations and rituals with festive Christmas designs.

Floral and classic images can beautifully support your wedding pages.

Add playful accents and bright colors to children's pages.

Rich colors, homespun patterns, and the classic symbols of autumn set the tone for harvest-time pages.

Flowers, lace, and little patterns combine for charming baby accents.

One of my favorite magazines is Mary Engelbreit's *Home Companion*. Each issue inspires me with its nostalgic topics of heart and home and collectibles, and its charming photographs and illustrations. Often there are wonderful borders on its pages. I can translate these borders to a scrapbook page easily by using a similarly patterned scrapbooking paper and other materials that create the same look.

The idea boards work the same way. You can take the look of one theme and adapt it to the theme you are using to end up with a design that is brand-new. You can also translate an idea you created for another page, altering it to fit a new theme.

Scrapbookers have translated these ideas hundreds of ways. One friend used the Thanksgiving table idea from the "Fall" idea board (page 112) and adapted it for her newborn daughter's "welcome home" page. The family had baked a special cake, so she silhouetted a photo of it and cut the tablecloth out of pink plaid paper.

Scrapbookers have translated the ribbon garlands shown on the "Our Baby Girl" (page 112) and "Merry Christmas" (page 110) idea boards numerous times. Scrapbookers have also translated the punched heart flower design from "Our Wedding" (page 111) on wedding, garden, Valentine's Day, and little girl pages. Notice also how I made the bottom left border on the "Our Baby Girl" idea board and the bottom right border on the "Die Cuts" idea board (page 89) similarly.

Another way you can translate ideas is by making a decorative accent in atypical colors that suit the theme of your page. I used leaves punched from soft pastel papers to make the top left border on the "Our Baby Girl" idea board.

Make Optimum Use of Your Scrapbooking Idea Resources

Stop to consider what it is that caused you to notice a particular page in a scrapbooking book or magazine, whether good photographs, nice color combinations, a balanced layout, or an inventive border.

Become a detective. Each page can offer you a mini lesson on some aspect of scrapbooking. Train yourself to look for the details. Dissect the pages a bit. Look for specific elements you can use, like unique matting, die cut usage, sticker combinations, and lettering style.

Keep a notebook or calendar to jot down ideas for a certain event or season. Note the issue and page where the idea was shown.

Size Adaptation

Perhaps you've seen a great idea for a scrapbook layout. The dimensions of the page as shown, however, are different from yours. Usually it is easy to adjust them to your format. There are several ways to do it:

Shift the pictures slightly to achieve a balanced look for the dimensions of the page. It might mean moving them closer, farther, higher, or lower on the page.

Use one less or one more picture to balance the layout.

Add or take out a die cut to help the spaces work better.

Change the size of a decorative element. For example, an airplane image can be found as a large die cut, a small die cut, or a sticker; use the one that will fit best on your page.

Notice how the images are scaled proportionately to suit the page dimensions yet keep the same mood and general layout.

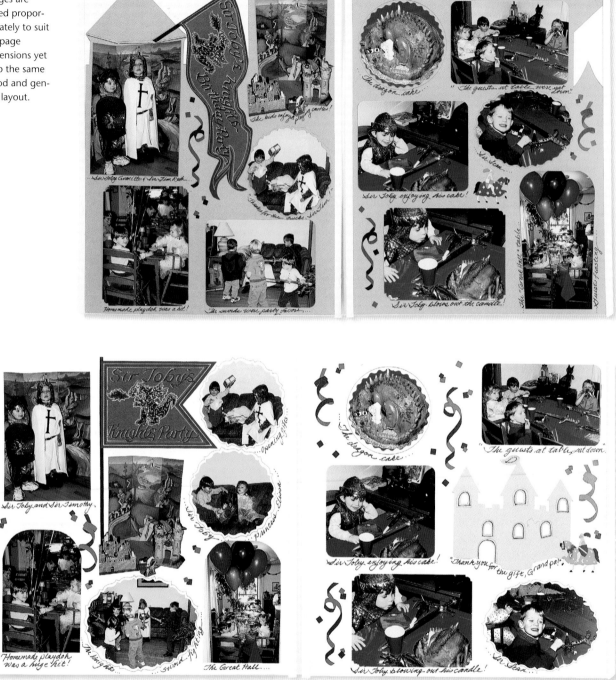

This last technique can be helpful if you are making similar books of different sizes. My friend Monica worked with this situation recently. She recorded many of the same events in books for her children, her father-in-law, and a great-aunt. Monica used a twelve-inch-by-fifteen-inch format for her children's books, a twelve-by-twelve for Grandpa Will's, and a ten-by-twelve for Aunt Lea's. She used the same general layout for all the books, simply scaling down the size of the symbols as needed. She also adjusted the amount of journaling and number of photographs to fit the books' sizes while maintaining the same basic layout for them all.

Capturing the Past

One of the most satisfying scrapbooking projects is that of working with your old family photographs. Nearly every family would like to have a heritage album to beautifully display the pictures and label them for the younger generations to learn from, connect with, and enjoy. Making a heritage album can be a rewarding experience. But it also has some challenges.

Depending on your age and the span of time your pictures cover, it may be difficult to record the details because many of the photos may have been taken before you were born and an eyewitness may no longer be alive to give details of the account. Perhaps you are fortunate and have letters or other documentation to explain the significance of certain events. If not, you will be working in third person and recording the events without having observed them. There are several ways to approach this situation.

First of all, you can record the information related to the events as it has been passed down orally in the family. Often, the stories evolve as time goes by, but the current version is still the most accurate one you will probably ever have. It is important to write it down before it gets forgotten completely. Or you can include the varying versions, identifying who described it each way.

Postcards of the town where the action takes place and from the appropriate era are a wonderful addition. These are often easy to find at antique shops and flea markets in the area. Look for postmarks on them to help determine accurate dates.

Correspondence reveals descriptions of daily life as well as handwriting. You should definitely include samples (in a protective sleeve).

Try to decorate the pages in your heritage scrapbook in a style that evolves as your subject moves through the decades, capturing the mood of the year.

Tip: Save your calendars! They are a wealth of information of activities and contacts and remind you of occasions that you might otherwise forget and that transpired around the same time frame. They are also great for providing extra pieces of information to fill in details of a particular season or year.

I had a mission in mind when I made my parents' heritage albums for their Christmas gift in 1997. I wanted to set family events in time. That is, rather than just showing the progression of the generations in the album, I wanted to mark the occurrence of historical events in context with the photographs. This approach can give us insight into how our family may have been affected by the developments of politics, science and technology, and culture. I found a relatively easy way to include this information.

I used a popular book titled *The Timetables of History* by Bernard Grun. It is a listing of key historical events arranged chronologically with seven subheadings for each year. This enables me to combine my family photographs, names and dates, memorabilia, and funny, touching, or inspiring stories in a year-by-year progression that can include

Use classic accents with your heritage photographs.

- news events
- popular music
- discoveries/inventions
- births/deaths/weddings
- popular toys
- fads
- popular slang
- movies
- art and literature
- radio and TV debuts

Since the book contains so many options, I chose entries that tied in with the interests, hobbies, and occupations of my family.

DETERMINING DATES

A common problem in making a heritage album is that the photographs you possess may not be dated. Of course, you want to include them in an accurate progression, so how can you do it?

Many photographs contain clues that can assist you in determining accurate dates—at least they can get you close. Look for the following clues:

- *Location—when did the family occupy that house?*
- *The license plates or model of a car*
- *Wedding rings*
- *Styles of hair, clothing, glasses, beards*
- *Room colors and furniture arrangements*
- *Photos displayed in the background*
- *A nonfamily guest in the photo that would indicate a certain visit you could easily pinpoint*
- *Business signs*
- *Size of trees, shrubs, or other landscape features*

Compare undated photographs with those that do have a date on them.

Identify the youngest person in the photo. What is his or her birth date? How old does he or she look in this picture? Simple addition will help you estimate a probable time frame.

Ask extended family members if they possess any labeled photos that might help identify faces in some of yours. One group shot with names noted can be the key to unlocking the identification for many other pictures.

Combine your old photographs with news events of the day, placing family events in time.

Label each photo as accurately as you can. If you think you know the year in which a photo was taken but aren't sure, label it by using the "approximately" symbol (≈). For photographs that really stump you, ask relatives or friends who might know or might be able to point you in the right direction. If you're still stumped, identify what you can and estimate the year, putting a question mark after it.

Encourage Children to Scrapbook

Have your kids (or nieces and nephews) exercise their creativity by starting to record their own stories while they are young. My son Alex flew to Washington, D.C., with my mother to spend Thanksgiving 1999 with my sister and brother-in-law. It was his first flight ever and his first trip there since he was a baby. We sent a disposable camera and encouraged him to take pictures of his trip. Larry and Marcia are always wonderful hosts, offering many outings in the historical area they call home. Before coming back, Alex and Marcia spent a day putting together a fabulous scrapbook of an eight-year-old's perspective of the city.

Afterword

We had been anticipating Christmas for months. We had recently wrapped three large identical boxes for Dad and Mom, plus a smaller gift to be given first. We positioned the presents carefully in various places in the house. A video camera, mounted on its tripod, was poised, ready to capture my parents' reactions to the special heritage albums we were about to present.

Three heritage albums that spanned 102 years (and six generations of relatives) marked our growth and celebrated our achievements.

January, February, and March of 1997 had been given to gathering all the family photos, sorting and labeling them, and filing them in chronological order. We spent a significant amount of time filling in the family tree with names and dates and gathering other pieces of information that might be helpful. We occupied April by organizing a filing system for the pieces we hoped to include in the albums and placing each piece in the proper file. In May, the albums began to take shape. My sister Laurie graciously crisscrossed town to make the necessary copies, while I began assembling pages. My sister Marcia continually spurred us on over long

Time passes quickly. Make good use of the opportunity you have to record your family's stories.

Happy 46th Anniversary

October 12, 1997

distance with her interest, encouraging words, and checks to help with the expenses. It took an all-out effort to compile a century of family history in twelve months!

Our parents were a bit puzzled when they opened the first gift—a box of Kleenex (we had a hunch they'd need it!). "You have so much," we told them. "We thought we'd just be practical this year." And so our Christmas morning began.

By day's end we had shared tears, laughter, and quiet reflection of our life as a family as they leafed through 300 pages of photos, souvenirs, and memories. The albums spanned just over one hundred years—1896 (the year my grandfather was born) through 1997. We had taken pictures all during the year to be sure the scrapbooks would be up-to-date. In October we posed Dad and Mom for these pictures snapped on their forty-sixth wedding anniversary, photos we might not otherwise have taken.

Time goes by more quickly than you might think. It is so easy to put off the opportunities of writing about your lives, hearing the stories of your elders, and recording the details that can be shared. I encourage you to make it a goal to work on. Prod your family members to get their memories on paper, audiotape, or videotape. Maybe one person can take on the effort by interviewing various relatives. A little research and the preparation of some thoughtful questions may reveal adventures you never dreamed your family had lived or the moments that turned their path a particular direction, often impacting the whole family.

Our parents spent many hours during the following months looking through these albums. I'm so glad we made them together when we did. My dad passed away unexpectedly on a beautiful, quiet morning in May 1998, having suffered a heart attack. I had hoped to fill in some of the pages with his perspective of the events we recorded. Unfortunately that won't happen. But I'm so thankful we have the memories of that wonderful Christmas Day and both of them sitting together, enjoying our gifts to them.

Appendix: Special Scrapbooking Issues

*I*n this appendix, you will find sections on photo safety, product safety, determining themes for your albums, a sample letter asking friends and family to make a page for a gift album, and strategies for fixing common scrapbooking mistakes.

What Is Photo-Safe?

Many factors can contribute to your photos becoming damaged. What can prevent it?

You will often see the terms *photo-safe* and *archival quality* on the labels of scrapbooking products. They seem to indicate that the product wouldn't damage your photographs in any way, but the use of these words is not regulated at this time and does not require scientific testing. Counting on these alone as an indication of quality can lead you to purchase a product believing it to be something it is not. When you shop, read the labeling information carefully, looking for more specific terminology.

Photographs that are not stored properly càn fade or discolor quickly.

There are efforts being made to clarify the archival issues of the photographic and paper industries, how they apply specifically to scrapbooking, and to communicate the information to the consumer with clear standards and accurate labeling. Watch for these standards to be set.

One point of clarity in the market is the *Photographic Activity Test* (P.A.T). This test determines whether a product will adversely affect a photograph. Many companies that manufacture or distribute scrapbooking supplies have had their products tested. Look for products that state the product has passed the P.A.T.

The P.A.T. does not, however, indicate longevity of the product itself. Particularly in your choice of album, use common sense to determine whether the album seems durable. Other criteria also come into play regarding a product's own life; for example, what makes a paper "permanent." The American National Standards Institute and the National Information Standards Organization (ANSI/NISO) define *permanent* as "the ability of paper to last at least several hundred years without significant deterioration under normal use and storage conditions in libraries and archives." You want the materials you include in your scrapbooks to be long-lasting and photo-safe even though your homes will not have the environmental controls of a library or museum.

The topic becomes technical very quickly, but reviewing the following definitions will help you understand the basics and get more protection for every scrapbook dollar you spend.

PHOTO-SAFETY DEFINITIONS

Acid-free: The pH scale ranges from 0 to 14. Zero to just below 7 is the acid side of the scale, 7 is pH neutral, and anything from just over 7 to and including 14 is alkaline. Materials having a pH level of 7.0 or above are considered acid-free. There are pH-testing pens on the market that enable you to check for acid in paper items you may want to include in your scrapbook (birthday cards, ticket stubs, and so on). These don't tell you how alkaline the paper is, however. To give you a context for the scale, lemon juice measures 3 and liquid bleach measures 11. Clearly, you want the products you use to be closer to the neutral point.

Buffered: *Buffering* is the result of a process by which paper pulp is treated to help bring it from an acid to a neutral or alkaline reading on the pH scale. Paper is most often treated with calcium carbonate to achieve this. Many acid-free papers are manufactured with an extra amount of calcium carbonate (or other buffering agent) to achieve a "buffering reserve." This is done to compensate for the natural deterioration of the paper, which slowly moves the paper back toward the acid side of the scale. Because of this, using buffered paper has been widely suggested in the industry, but some archival experts actually recommend using unbuffered paper with colored photographs. Buffered paper should never touch the *front* of a photograph, as it is thought to cause deterioration of the top layer of the picture. If your album's pages or the decorative papers you include are buffered (and many are), using page protectors is important. The most conservative suggestion is to try to stay as close to neutral on the pH scale with anything that has contact with your photographs.

Lignin-free: Paper with the lignin extracted to 1 percent or less is considered *lignin-free. Lignin* is an organic substance found in plants. If not removed during the papermaking process of wood pulp paper, its presence can cause the paper to discolor and potentially break down, as well as cause photographic staining. (The lignin found in cotton plants has a much less drastic effect, so cotton paper is preferable.) Since most of the paper available to scrapbookers is wood pulp–based, purchasing lignin-free paper is important.

PVC-free: *PVC-free* indicates plastic that is free of polyvinylchlorides. PVCs emit gases that can have a very damaging effect on photographs. This term applies to the clear sleeves used to protect the finished pages in your album, the pockets made to hold memorabilia, or the outer covering of the album itself. I've seen some plastic products made for scrapbooking that say "acid-free" on the label. *Acid* is not a term that applies to plastics, so look for other PVC-related terminology. The product may not say "PVC-free" but will be if made of polypropylene, polyethylene, or polyester (Mylar).

Product Safety Basics

What about the safety factors of other products you will use in your albums?

PENS AND INKS

Because *acid-free* is the term that so many look for as the safety stamp of approval for scrapbooking products, it is on many pens. Actually the term doesn't really pertain here. According to a leading researcher of archival information related to scrapbooks, by the time your ink has dried on the page, the acid level present is immeasurable. Instead, the key consideration here is the ingredient that colors the ink. Some inks are a water-based dye that may fade over time. Instead look for pens containing pigment ink. Pigments adhere to the paper rather than staining it as dyes do. They provide better sharpness and contrast. Other positive descriptions you can look for in regard to pens are *fade-proof, lightfast,* and *waterproof.* If you like to stamp your pages with rubber-stamping products, look for pigment ink stamp pads as well.

ADHESIVES

The primary rule of conservators in their handling of materials is "Never do something you can't undo." Hold older photos and irreplaceable documents in your scrapbook in PVC-free sleeves or with acid-free mounting corners made from paper or a safe plastic. This will give you the option of removing them to make copies at a later time and enable you to view the back of a document. And making a copy of the original to use in your album will allow you more creative options.

Many scrapbooking adhesives are permanent. Assuming that you are approaching your scrapbook as a permanent compilation, you may want to use a permanent adhesive. First, however, consider whether you have the negatives or other copies of the pictures.

Use only acid-free adhesives. There are a variety of types to choose from. Tapes come by the roll, in small square tabs, or in a dispenser in tiny sections perfect for using on die cuts. Glue sticks and glue pens are also available. I have had better success using tape to hold paper to the page but know many scrapbookers who use the other methods and have been quite satisfied with the results. Never use rubber cement in your scrapbooks!

DIE CUTS

If you buy prepackaged die cuts, check for information on the label that will tell you the quality of the paper from which they were made. Shops offering die cuts sold by the piece will most likely have someone on hand who can provide that information. If you use a die cut machine to make your own, use the best-quality paper available.

STICKERS

Most stickers, even those not labeled "acid-free" or "photo-safe," have been found to be within acceptable pH levels. Most will quite likely be fine to use on your pages. However, it is prudent to look for stickers that have safety information noted on their packaging.

ALBUMS

When choosing the album itself, consider the safety factors for the varying elements used (pages, plastic pockets, and cover materials) along with looking to see if it seems to be constructed well.

PHOTOCOPIES

Color photocopies offer you the ability to make inexpensive copies of the pictures or documents you may want to include in your scrapbooks. They are also a great tool for changing the size of something you would like to include. Although the copies may be of a bit less visual quality than the original, they are considered to be more stable than the original photographs. This simply means that the color will stay true for a longer time.

Laser copies are safe to use in your albums with regular photographs. But the process that causes the toner to adhere to the copy paper is a heat process, and heat exposure to the copy can also cause the toner to lift back *off* of the paper. Thus, as a precaution, keep copied material in a cool environment.

There is another way to make a copy of a photo if you don't have the negative. Many photo shops have machines capable of making a print on photographic paper without having the negative. It produces an eight by ten, so the machine can reproduce more than one standard-size photo at one time on a single piece of this paper for a reasonable price. Stay acquainted with the available services at your local camera shop or developing station. Computer technology is also offering increasingly good options in photo reproduction.

ASK THE MANUFACTURER

Don't hesitate to call a manufacturer's headquarters to ask questions about their scrapbooking products. Company names and city locations are listed on most product packaging. Their telephone numbers are easy to track down by calling information. Advertisements in scrapbooking magazines typically list contact information as well. Surprisingly, several companies I contacted had better archival quality than they noted on their packaging.

It is my hope that manufacturers and distributors will have their products P.A.T. tested and clearly mark their packaging with pertinent archival information so that informed consumers can make educated choices. Since many products do not carry that information at this time, I have compiled a large notebook of general archival information and definitions, copies of the applicable standards and documents for imaging materials and paper permanence, and specifications for the products I use. The manufacturers' contact listing in the Source Guide provides some of this information. I hope this kind of information becomes available at all scrapbooking shops.

There are a few other threats to photos' and scrapbooks' safety that you should consider. They are by far the factors that *most* affect the life of your photographs. These enemies of a scrapbook are sunlight, humidity (aim for a consistent 30 to 40 percent), warm temperatures (keep from drastic fluctuations), insects (some feed on scrapbook-type materials), stress (handle your albums carefully), and grape jelly (train your darlings to wash their hands before sitting down to look at their albums).

Be aware that photography and wood pulp paper are relatively recent developments, having been around only since the latter part of the 1800s. Many advancements have been made in their sciences, but much will be revealed about their · longevity simply by the passing of time.

Of course you want to compile and care for your albums well, but do not be afraid to have them out often, enjoying them to the fullest and letting the stories enrich your family bonds.

Album Themes

The type of album you choose to make will set you on your course, enabling you to begin focusing on the unique aspects the subject holds and the possibilities of specifics you can capture on the pages. You will most likely decide on a subject that triggers a natural affection and around which you have a large storehouse of fond memories. The following are some ideas of various approaches you can take.

■ **Family album**—You may begin with your most recent photos and work backward and forward. This all-inclusive album will replace your existing photo albums.

■ **Wedding**—The album's decorative style should reflect the style of the wedding. Start with the earliest available photos of the couple together and work chronologically through dating, courtship, bridal showers, and so on, all the way through the blessed day. Include a page telling how the couple met, in their own words if possible.

■ **Child's birth and development**—Include events that occurred during the pregnancy (news and family activities) and follow along to tell the child's story. At each birthday, write down the child's interests, favorite things, and daily routine. Occasionally let your child create a page. Your child's artwork and writing at different stages will be a treasure, and he (or she) can observe his own progress.

■ **Adoption**—This album can begin with the baby's arrival or include the process of longing (and disappointments) that led to the adoption of this special child. Fill in the album with milestones in the baby's development and the special moments this family enjoys.

■ **Holidays**—Record the activities of the holiday that gathers in the most family members. Include traditions, recipes, and religious significance.

■ **Vacations**—Make a "road map" throughout the entire itinerary. Include the plans, the route, special places and activities, surprises that occurred along the way, and photos of the vehicle (inside and out!).

■ **Reunion**—Include photos of various groupings, memories of past times, and special events to celebrate the get-together. Use "then and now" photos of an individual on the same page. An oldest/youngest combination photo (a great-grandmother holding her new great-grandchild, for example) is special. Have pens available for everyone to add signatures, artwork, information, comments, or stories.

- **Heritage**—Track down as much family history as you can. Gather photos and any written information you have available. Begin with the courtship or childhoods of your anchor couple. Record the progression year by year including local and world news events in your notations. It will place the family members in time and give you insight into how their lives may have been impacted.

- **Graduation, anniversary, special birthday, or retirement**—Have friends and family members each contribute a page to commemorate any of these events. Compile the pages into an album that will be a treasured gift.

- **Alphabet**—Help a preschooler learn his or her letters with an album that includes the child's own family, friends, and favorite places. Use names of schools, your street or neighborhood, and locations of sports activities, stores, and restaurants you frequently visit. Remember to include pets and favorite toys.

- **School days**—Follow a child's academic year. Entries can include artwork, field trips, teachers' and special friends' names, and a picture of the child's school. Reduce large papers, report cards, and handwritten stories on a copier to save space or photograph them to include in smaller form.

- **Memory/tribute**—Making this kind of album can help you grieve and heal from the loss of a loved one. You can compile it from your own special memories, or approach it as a contribution album and have other family members and friends make pages also.

- **Monthly or seasonal calendar**—Cover just one year or several, depending on how many activities you want to include. This is a great way to focus on the regular family activities rather than just the special events. Include pictures of the children enjoying the first flowers of spring, raking autumn leaves, and shoveling snow.

- **"Capture the Family"**—Make a two-page spread per person highlighting his or her interests and some details of his or her life. Include pictures of each person at several different ages. (See "Capture the Family," page 51, for ideas on this.)

- **"A Day in the Life"**—A small-sized album works well here. Compile a quick-to-assemble book recording your *normal* routine. Show work areas, appliances, car, other pertinent items. You could also make an album titled "A Week in the Life," to include daily work, household, and weekend activities.

- **History of a business, church, or organization**—Interview available members/participants (especially charter members, if possible) for their perspectives and memories and to double-check details for accuracy.

- **Cookbook**—A small-sized album is nice for this project. For a family who spends a lot of time in the kitchen together, this can be an easy way of recording favorite recipes and times the recipes are traditionally served. Include the year you began making each dish and who brought it to the family. This is a great gift for a soon-to-be daughter-in-law.

- **"Insults-R-Us"**—This is more of a booklet but makes a humorous birthday card lovingly poking fun at the recipient. Use candid shots, add funny captions, or find pictures from magazines to incorporate in a clever message.

- **A Child's Garden of Verses**—The selections of Robert Louis Stevenson's wonderful book of poetry will be a lovely framework for an album containing photos of your children that relate to the topic. This is a wonderful way to include childhood pictures from several generations in a combined, nonchronological manner. It would make a great gift for a grandmother!

Sample Letter for Contribution Album

To request contributions of album pages from family and friends that would be used to create a scrapbook for my daughter, I sent out this letter. The response was great.

March 13, 1997

Dear Family and Friends,

This spring will mark Jacie's graduation from high school. We are so proud of her! We are pulling together a gift that will capture special memories with important people in her life—You among them! We hope you can participate.

The project: We have purchased a scrapbook and would like you to decorate a page that we can compile with the others and present to her at her graduation party on May 25. Make your page as simple or fancy as you like.

Some Ideas: A photo of you . . . photo of Jacie . . . better yet, a photo of you with Jacie. A poem, the words of a favorite song, a favorite scripture passage, a written or pictured account of a memory you have of her or an experience you've shared, cutout pictures glued collage-style. Decorate it with stickers, a colored border, sketches, or cartoon drawings. Use a combination of ideas or come up with your own! If you are a family, you could mark the page into blocks and have each person decorate a section. And please sign your name on your page.

Please send us your page by May 12. Thanks for your help with this project and especially for the contribution you have made in Jacie's life. We know your page will be a treasure to her for years to come. If you have any questions, please call us at . . .

Blessings to you all!

To make it as easy as possible for folks to participate, we included a blank scrapbook page, this letter, and two stamped envelopes: one addressed to the next person to receive the page (so they could complete the other side of the scrapbook page) and that included their instruction sheet, and another addressed to us for the return mailing.

You could ask each person to make his or her page on an 8½-by-11-inch sheet and mount it on a larger page, or slide the page into a protective sleeve in a binder-style album.

Oops!

Sometimes a scrapbooking project doesn't go as smoothly as you'd like. Below are some typical mishaps and fixes for each.

THE ONLY PHOTO I HAVE OF AN IMPORTANT EVENT OR MOMENT IS A CRUMMY SHOT!

Caption it with a funny quote or give details to explain why it is important. My mom baked *nine* cakes for my husband's fortieth birthday party, but the only picture I had of them together was blurry. I captioned it with a comment about the photographer's probably being on a sugar high.

I SKIPPED AN IMPORTANT EVENT

Add the page featuring the skipped event to the album as close to the correct spot as possible. Note the date of the event clearly. If you need something to fill the other side of the added page, try

a collage of photos from the same general time period

news events from the time (laid out as a newspaper page)

a seasonal summary with lots of decorative touches

a vacation or outing, with itinerary and map

I ACCIDENTALLY SKIPPED A PAGE, WHICH NOW LEAVES AN EMPTY SPACE

See "I skipped an important event."

THERE'S A SPILL, STAIN, OR SCRIBBLE ON MY PAGE

Cover the offense with a photo, die cut, or sticker.

Add a piece of memorabilia.

Keep a sense of humor! This is now part of your story. Label what the mark is and who made it.

I HATE THE PAGE I'VE JUST COMPLETED!

Add a few small stickers or ink designs to tie it together better. Or, if nothing is on the back, trim the photos off and start over. If something is on the back, try to carefully lift the photos, mat the page with a piece of paper to cover any marks, and start again. Or—smile, learn, and live with it!

I'VE JUST MADE AN ERROR IN MY JOURNALING

Cover the area (if small), using a white opaque marker, and then rewrite it correctly. Or write the information on a piece of paper or on a die cut and place it over the error.

Source Guide

Sources for Supplies and Products

The following is a chapter-by-chapter listing of sources for the scrapbooking products used in the photos of this book. Some other products were photographed with the scrapbooking supplies for aesthetic purposes only and therefore are not listed here.

Permission was granted by each of the companies to use photographs of their products throughout the book. Some of the companies requested that a separate copyright notice also be included. The notices below are for companies that are listed more than once in "Sources for Supplies and Products." All other notices are included with their respective product listing.

Accu-Cut: Designs © Accu-Cut Systems. All rights reserved. Worldwide Rights Reserved.

Ellison: Designs are copyrights and trademarks of Ellison.

The Gifted Line: The Gifted Line © Michel & Co. From the John Grossman Collection of Antique Images.

The Paper Patch: Patterned papers copyright © The Paper Patch.

CHAPTER 1

***The Myers Brothers*, page 1**
Paper corners: Pebbles in My Pocket

CHAPTER 2

***Jacie*, page 7**
Die cut: Ellison
Template: lettering is "Linzi's Calligraphy Lower," by Trace-It-Up from Cut-It-Up
Patterned paper: The Paper Patch
Stencil: pine trees © All Night Media, Inc.

Barber Shop, **page 8**
Die cut: Ellison
Stickers: letters by Mrs. Grossman's
Punch: Family Treasures

Supplies on Cart, **page 13**
Decorative scissors: Fiskars
Die cuts: football player by Accu-Cut; all others by Ellison
Paper cutter, 12″: Fiskars
Pens: Zig Memory System Writer by EK Success; Micron and Gelly Roll by Sakura
Punches: Family Treasures
Stickers: Mrs. Grossman's
Templates: Extra Special Products and Pebbles in My Pocket

Supplies on Desk, **page 14**
Circle cutter and oval cutter: Fiskars
Craft knife: C-Thru
Flexible curve: C-Thru
Pens: Zig Memory System Calligraphy and Zig Memory System Scroll & Brush by
     EK Success; Callipens by Sakura
Rubber stamps: Personal Stamp Exchange
Templates: Extra Special Products; Border Buddy by EK Success

CHAPTER 3

Wedding Day/65th Anniversary, **page 17**
Stencil: source unknown
Template: banners from Extra Special Products

Flower Child, **page 18**
Patterned paper: The Paper Patch
Stickers: camera and flowers by Mrs. Grossman's; letters by Deja Views

1 Year Old, **page 19**
Die cuts: cake with icing by Accu-Cut; bow by Pebbles in My Pocket
Patterned paper: The Paper Patch

The First Time . . . , **page 19**
Stickers: Mrs. Grossman's

Romeo and Juliet Mice, **page 20**
Stickers: Mrs. Grossman's
Tree, bushes, and balcony are hand cut by the author

Laurie Jayne Arrives, **page 24**
Die cut: Creative Memories
Stickers: Bryce & Madeline

Gorman Nature Center, **page 26**
Sketches adapted from illustrations by Gordon Morrison appearing in *The Curious
     Naturalist*. A Spectrum Book, © 1980 Prentice Hall Inc., Artwork © 1977 and 1978
     by the Massachusetts Audubon Society.

Snow Play, **page 27**
Die cut: Accu-Cut
Punch: Family Treasures

Christmas 1959, **page 28**
Patterned paper: The Paper Patch

CHAPTER 4

Hazel Irene Moses, **page 31**
Die cuts: Ellison
Patterned paper: The Paper Patch

Memorabilia, **page 32**
Sticker: Mrs. Grossman's

Chicken Pox, **page 33**
Die cuts: Pebbles in My Pocket
Patterned paper: The Paper Patch
Stickers: letters by Pebbles in My Pocket

1942 Map and Postcard, **page 33**
Map paper: source unknown

CHAPTER 5

Great-Grandmother on Porch Swing, **page 41**
Patterned paper: The Paper Patch
Photo corners: Canson

Childhood Is . . . , **page 43**
Punches: Family Treasures (the dark leaves were made by punching paper in the shape
   of a heart and then cutting the heart in half)
Lettering style by Melissa Phillips

Tooth Fairy, **page 44**
Decorative scissors: Fiskars
Die cuts: castle by Accu-Cut; tooth and mountain by Pebbles in My Pocket
Patterned paper: The Paper Patch
Punch: small circle by Fiskars
Stickers: Mrs. Grossman's

Letter to Santa, **page 45**
Decorative scissors: Fiskars
Patterned paper: The Paper Patch

Jenna in Flowers, **page 45**
Decorative scissors: Fiskars
Die cuts: flowers and leaves by Pebbles in My Pocket
Punch: swirl by Family Treasures
Stickers: Mrs. Grossman's
Template: flowers by Extra Special Products

Thomas Jefferson, **page 47**
Photographs of Thomas Jefferson's scrapbook pages are copyright © Monticello/Thomas Jefferson Foundation, Inc.

Edna Mae, **page 49**
Die cuts: schoolhouse by Ellison; signpost by Pebbles in My Pocket
Stickers: water pump, shoe, rocking chair, wood stove, and farm animals by Creative Memories; "Congratulations" banner, mortarboard, and diploma by Frances Meyer; letter blocks, gardening-related items, hat, and butterfly by The Gifted Line; landscape, bag of groceries, harvest border, winter wear, money, turkey, peach, and grapes by Mrs. Grossman's

John and Anita's Wedding, **page 50**
Stickers: Frances Meyer

CHAPTER 6

You Are the Apple of My Eye, **page 55**
Die cuts: Ellison
Patterned paper: The Paper Patch
Stickers: Mrs. Grossman's; letters by Deja Views

Thank God I'm a Country Boy, **page 56**
Templates: circles and ovals by Extra Special Products

Rollin' and a Strollin', **page 57**
Decorative scissors: Fiskars
Lyrics to "Rollin' and a Strollin'" by Dana Ward, Cheshire Recordings

Baking Cookies, **page 58**
Die cut: gingerbread boy, source unknown
Stickers: Mrs. Grossman's
Bowl and bags are hand cut by author

Tea for Two, **page 59**
Decorative scissors: Fiskars
Paper: Canson Mi-Tentes, orchid
Stickers: Mrs. Grossman's
Teacups and teapot are hand cut by author

Cade: Any Way You Look at It, **page 61**
Card: source unknown
Patterned paper: The Paper Patch

CHAPTER 7

Snowman, **page 65**
Die cut: snowflake by Accu-Cut
Punches: Family Treasures

Matting Idea Boards, **pages 68 and 69**
Decorative scissors: Fiskars
Die cuts: Ellison
Patterned paper: The Paper Patch
Punch: Family Treasures
Stickers: letters along the top and sides are by Frances Meyer; "Cade" letters by Pebbles in My Pocket; all others by Mrs. Grossman's

Happy Easter, page 76
Decorative scissors: Fiskars
Stickers: Mrs. Grossman's
Basket, bow, and large eggs are handmade by author

Grace Elizabeth Feia, page 77
Patterned paper: The Paper Patch
Punch: Family Treasures
Decorative scissors: source unknown

Pumpkins, page 78
Patterned paper: The Paper Patch
Punches: Family Treasures

You're a Grand Old Flag, page 78
Patterned paper: The Paper Patch
Flag is hand cut by author

Color Combinations, page 79
Punches: Family Treasures
Stickers: Mrs. Grossman's
Template: wavy lines are "Clean-up/Bedtime" Pebbles Theme Tracer by Pebbles in My
    Pocket

CHAPTER 8

Scrapbooking Materials, page 82
Decorative scissors: Fiskars
Pens: Zig Memory System by EK Success; Callipens and Micron by Sakura
Punches: hand-held punches by Fiskars; all others by Family Treasures
Rubber stamps: Personal Stamp Exchange
Other items: sources unknown

Nassau, Bahamas, page 83
Die cuts: anchor, camera, fish, shells, sand dollar, and palm tree by Ellison; fins, sea-
    weed, and snorkel and mask by Pebbles in My Pocket
Stickers: Mrs. Grossman's

The Hickinbothams, est. 1976, page 84
Stickers: Mrs. Grossman's
Paper pieces for house are hand cut by author

Wedding Candles, page 84
Die cuts: bows (adapted to fit the page) by Ellison
Other paper pieces are hand cut by artist

Cousins, page 84
Stickers: Mrs. Grossman's

Kyle, page 85
Die cuts: Ellison
Stencil: letters are "Funky" by EK Success
Stickers: Mrs. Grossman's

Bath Time, page 86
Patterned paper: The Paper Patch
Punches: circles by Family Treasures
Templates: "Clean-up/Bedtime" Pebbles Theme Tracer by Pebbles in My Pocket

Corn, July 1998, **page 86**
Die cut: seed packet by Pebbles in My Pocket
Patterned paper: The Paper Patch
Scissors, scalloped edge: Fiskars
Stickers: Bryce & Madeline; letters by Deja View
Paper corn image is hand cut by author

Borders, Dots, and More, **page 87**
Decorative scissors: Fiskars
Die cuts: holly and bow by Accu-Cut; bee, flowers, and fish by Ellison; ant by Pebbles in
    My Pocket
Patterned paper: The Paper Patch
Punches: leaf, small geometric shapes, and snowflake by Family Treasures
Stickers: vehicles by Bryce & Madeline; pansy border by The Gifted Line; bows,
    Christmas-related items, confetti, flowers in "and," micro hearts, and micro flowers
    by Mrs. Grossman's; bridal shower by Frances Meyer; letters and numbers by
    Pebbles in My Pocket
Templates: triangle/circle border, checkerboard, butterfly, flowers on vine, wave, and
    grass edge by Pebbles in My Pocket

Cartoon Accents, **page 88**
Stickers: Mrs. Grossman's

January 2000, **page 89**
Die cuts: Ellison
Patterned paper: The Paper Patch
Punch: small circle by Family Treasures

Die Cuts Idea Board, **page 89**
Die cuts: premade border by Accu-Cut; rose and rose leaves by Crafty Cutter; airplane,
    letters, cityscape, fruit slice, jelly beans, mailbox, moose, snowflake, sun, teapot,
    and tiny leaves by Ellison; BBQ, beach chair, flower leaves, funky shapes, grass bor-
    der, ice cream cone, Popsicle, sunglasses, twig frame, and wading pool by Pebbles
    in My Pocket
Patterned paper: The Paper Patch
Punches: circle, maple leaf, and oak leaf by Family Treasures
Stickers: on teapot by Frances Meyer; in cityscape and with mailbox by Mrs.
    Grossman's

Stickers Idea Board, **page 90**
Die cut: director's chair by Ellison
Patterned paper: The Paper Patch
Stickers: premade corners and child throwing snowball by Bryce & Madeline; heritage
    items by Creative Memories; popcorn, tickets, movie reel, movie clapper, baby
    blocks, nursery-rhyme characters, and "stickers" letters by Frances Meyer; insects
    by The Gifted Line; amusement park, black-and-white border, Christmas scene,
    crayons, fish, gardening-related items, "Grandpa and John" letters, micro butter-
    flies, micro flowers, micro stars, pencils, pens, praying mantis, sewing-related
    items, snack food, sun, moon, stars, and tools by Mrs. Grossman's

Time Line, **page 91**
Stickers: Mrs. Grossman's

CHAPTER 9

Scrapbooking Tools, **page 92**
Circle cutter: Fiskars
Flexible curve: C-Thru
Punch: Family Treasures
Stencils: "A" and "H" are "Monogram Magic" by Delta Technical Coatings
Other items: sources unknown

Popsicle Shop, **page 93**
Decorative scissors: Fiskars
Die cuts: Pebbles in My Pocket
Patterned paper: The Paper Patch
Stickers: lettering by Pebbles in My Pocket
Template: edge used on yellow checked paper is "Borders #3" by Pebbles in My Pocket

All-Star Daddy, **page 94**
Stickers: Mrs. Grossman's
Template: stars by Extra Special Products

Robert Neil Hickinbotham, **page 95**
Template: "Romantic" Border Buddy by EK Success

Jenna Dancing, **page 95**
Stickers: Mrs. Grossman's
Dotted ribbon technique by Connie Fintel. (Use a fairly wide wave template; draw once, then move template down and to the left a bit to create the second side of the ribbon. To make solid black section, fill in the tiniest space it creates; add ink dots for a 3-D effect.)

Muscle Men, **page 96**
Decorative scissors: Fiskars
Patterned paper: The Paper Patch
Stickers: letters by Deja View
Template: circles by Extra Special Products
Geometric shapes are hand cut by author

Marcia, Laurie, Anita, 1957, **page 97**
Decorative scissors: Fiskars
Die cuts: Ellison

Wedding Cake, **page 98**
Die cut: Ellison
Punch: Family Treasures

Traffic, **page 99**
Stickers: Mrs. Grossman's

Special Delivery, **page 100**
Die cut: Ellison
Patterned paper: The Paper Patch
Stamp: Personal Stamp Exchange

***Donald Dawson Myers*, page 100**
Paper: Canson
Stamps: Old typesetting dingbats purchased at an antique shop
Stickers: Frances Meyer

CHAPTER 10

***Girls in Hats*, page 103**
Stickers: Mary Engelbreit by Creative Imaginations © ME Ink. Stickers used with permission of Mary Engelbreit Studios. All rights reserved.
Feathers are hand cut by author

***Our "Big" Snow*, page 104**
Patterned paper: source unknown

***Brookside Gardens*, page 104**
Stickers: Mrs. Grossman's

***A Joyful Eastertide*, page 104**
Decorative scissors: source unknown
Punches: circle and teardrop, source unknown

***Lia Gabrielle Hickinbotham*, page 106**
Pen: silver fine point by Sakura
All images hand cut by author

***Gifts for Lia*, page 107**
Stickers: clothes and basket by Mrs. Grossman's; pig by Bryce & Madeline

***Heritage Idea Board (Moments in Time)*, page 109**
Die cuts: birds, bows, mini flowers by Accu-Cut
Patterned paper: The Paper Patch
Stickers: women's accessories by Creative Memories; baby-related items and raspberries by Frances Meyer; fruit, pansy and pansy border, travel-related items, roses, forget-me-not border, tea set, and lilacs (at bottom right) by The Gifted Line; wedding lace border and floral/bow, "Paper Whispers" embroidery, peach bow, "Moments in Time" letters and "1920" numbers, individual flowers (at bottom right) by Mrs. Grossman's
Templates: circles and ovals by Extra Special Products; large swirl designs (shown in ink and cut from paper) are "Romantic" Border Buddy by EK Success

***Winter Idea Board*, page 109**
Die cuts: trees and mountain landscape (at bottom right) by Accu-Cut; speed skater, skier, and ski jumper by Crafty Cutter; cupid, house, "love you" letters, mittens, rose, shamrock, snowflakes, snowmen, and bare tree by Ellison; baking equipment, mug, fir tree (behind large snowman), primitive hearts, scalloped heart, ski gear, and snowmobile by Pebbles in My Pocket
Patterned paper: The Paper Patch
Punch: snowflake by Family Treasures
Stickers: toddlers by Bryce & Madeline; "St. Patrick's Day" letters by Deja Views; all others by Mrs. Grossman's

Summer Vacation Idea Board, page 110

Die cuts: maple leaf and beach landscape by Accu-Cut; airplane, cactus, covered wagon, log cabin, Statue of Liberty, U.S.A. map, and world landmarks by Ellison; BBQ, car, cityscape, fishing fly and fishing pole, four-wheeler, picnic basket, pine tree, shade tree, twig frame, and wave runner by Pebbles in My Pocket

Patterned paper: The Paper Patch

Stickers: toddlers by Bryce & Madeline; beach-related items around "The Beach," rope border behind title, and travel-related items (in upper-left corner border) by Frances Meyer; ticket border and taxi by The Gifted Line; forest animals and picnic items by Mrs. Grossman's; "Summer and Vacation," "Canada," and "Touring the USA" letters by Deja Views; "The Beach" letters by Pebbles in My Pocket

Template: "The Beach" background is "Waterfun" Pebbles Theme Tracer by Pebbles in My Pocket

Christmas Idea Board, page 110

Die cuts: starburst by Crafty Cutter; open book, bow, candy cane, Christmas lights, Christmas tree, houses (gold paper added behind houses to make "lighted" windows), jingle bells, poinsettias, reindeer, sleigh, and tiny trees by Ellison; gingerbread kids and stocking by Pebbles in My Pocket

Patterned paper: The Paper Patch

Punches: heart by Family Treasures; bow on gingerbread girl, source unknown

Rubber stamps: holly border and pine bough by Personal Stamp Exchange

Stickers: angels, bows, candy cane, Christmas rush, holly, presents, and wreath by Mrs. Grossman's; letters by Pebbles in My Pocket

Templates: ornament from "Christmas #1" by Deja Views; leaves (to make ribbon border) by Extra Special Products

Manger and hay are hand cut by author

Wedding Idea Board, page 111

Die cuts: Irish wedding symbol, trellises, and "Simply Scherenschnitte" oval around "The Vows" by Accu-Cut; doves and bows and wedding cake by Ellison; laser-cut vine border (under limousine) by Pebbles in My Pocket

Patterned paper: The Paper Patch

Punch: heart by Family Treasures

Stamp: ring stamp by Personal Stamp Exchange

Stickers: all wedding-related items at bottom-right border by Frances Meyer; tulips, wrought iron gate, ribbons and packages (at upper-left corner), flowers and bow around "The Vows," ivy and flowers (in center), the bow in "The Bouquet," floral heart in "Tom and Mary," laser-cut narrow strips (on bottom-right corner), ribbon and roses in top-right border, and all sticker letters by Mrs. Grossman's; flowers with the doves, flowers in "The Bouquet," and all florals in "The Rings" by The Gifted Line

Templates: "A" monogram by Delta Technical Coatings; limousine by Extra Special Products

Let's Play Idea Board, page 111

Die cuts: paper-doll clothes by Accu-Cut; hands, hat with ribbon, swing set, tree, and tulips by Ellison; sliding board and purse by Pebbles in My Pocket

Patterned paper: The Paper Patch

Stickers: children (in top-right border) by Bryce & Madeline; all others by Mrs. Grossman's
Template: heart by Extra Special Products

Fall Idea Board, page 112
Die cuts: Indian by Crafty Cutter; barn, corn ear, cornucopia, crayon box, crayons, maple leaves, oak leaf, pennant, pilgrim man, pilgrim woman, pumpkin, scarecrow, and bare tree by Ellison; apple, back of school bus, football, football helmet, pencil, and ruler by Pebbles in My Pocket
Patterned paper: The Paper Patch
Punches: circle, maple leaf, and oak leaf by Family Treasures
Stamps: leaf borders by Personal Stamp Exchange
Stickers: school babies and fall babies by Bryce & Madeline; pig and rooster by Frances Meyer; apples, leaves, school supplies, and turkey by Mrs. Grossman's

Our Baby Girl Idea Board, page 112
Die cuts: bows under "Our Baby Girl" by Accu-Cut; baby carriage, moon, rose, stars, sun, teddy bear, and tulips by Ellison; baby bottle, baby foot, baby rattle, bootie, counting sheep, crib, diaper pin, ducky, and stork and bundle by Pebbles in My Pocket
Decorative scissors: Fiskars (to make outside edge of lacy border)
Doily: Pebbles in My Pocket
Patterned paper: The Paper Patch
Punches: circle (for baby faces and in geometric border), heart (cut in half to make baby ears), and maple leaf by Family Treasures; heart in lacy border by Fiskars; tiny bow, source unknown
Stickers: babies by Bryce & Madeline; pink magnolias under "Our Baby Girl" by Frances Meyer; micro flowers in "Jenna" and stork's bow by Mrs. Grossman's
Templates: bear/ribbon border (in lower-right corner) and "Our Baby Girl" lettering by Delta Technical Coatings; baby hand, leaf shape (incorporated in ribbon border in top-right corner) by Extra Special Products

Banner/Castle 12 × 15, page 114
Decorative scissors: source unknown
Paper: Canson
Stickers: confetti and knight on horse by Mrs. Grossman's; dragon, source unknown

Banner/Castle 12 × 12, page 114
Decorative scissors: source unknown
Die cut: castle by Accu-Cut
Paper: Canson
Stickers: confetti by Mrs. Grossman's; dragon, source unknown

Banner/Castle 10 × 12, page 115
Die cut: castle, source unknown
Paper: Canson
Stickers: confetti and knight on horse by Mrs. Grossman's; dragon is "Stickopotamus" by EK Success

1924 Wedding, **page 116**
Die cuts: heart and rings by Canson
Paper: Canson
Stickers: pink magnolias (at bottom-left corner) by Frances Meyer; hearts and violet
     border by The Gifted Line

1954 Blocks, **page 117**
Sticker: baby rattle by Mrs. Grossman's

AFTERWORD

Chapter opener, **page 118**
Album: Creative Memories
Decorative scissors: source unknown

Happy 46th Anniversary, **page 120**
Stickers: R. A. Lang Card Co.

Manufacturers' Contact and Archival Information

The following companies manufacture products that are shown in photographs
of supplies or were used in creating the scrapbook pages and idea boards. If applicable, the archival quality information that pertains to a specific product is provided.
"Not applicable" means that a tool or other item (such as decorative scissors, punches,
and templates) was used to *make* the page; it was not actually *placed onto* the page.

3L Corp.
685 Chaddick Dr.
Wheeling, IL 60090
(800) 828-3130
www.3Lcorp.com

Archival information: Acid-free, P.A.T. passed

Accu-Cut Systems
1035 E. Dodge St.
Fremons, NE 68026
(800) 288-1670
www.accucut.com

Archival information for Simply Scherenschnitte: acid-free, lignin-free, pH 9.13,
calcium carbonate minimum 2%, meets ANSI/NISO standards for paper permanence

All Night Media, Inc.
454 Du Bois St.
San Rafael, CA 94912
(800) STAMPED (782-6733)
www.allnightmedia.com

Archival information: not applicable

Bryce & Madeline Stickers, see *Creative Imaginations*

C-Thru Ruler Company
6 Britton Dr.
Bloomfield, CT 06002
(860) 243-0303
www.cthruruler.com

Archival information for letter stickers: acid-free

Canson, Inc.
21 Industrial Dr.
South Hadley, MA 01075
(413) 538-9250
www.canson-us.com

Archival information: photo corners are acid-free; papers are P.A.T. passed

Cheshire Recordings
P.O. Box 49
Rackerby, CA 95972
(888) 679-2297
website unknown

Archival information: not applicable

Crafty Cutter
P.O. Box 430
San Miguel, CA 93451
(805) 467-2664
website unknown

Archival information for die cuts: acid-free, lignin-free, buffered

Creative Imaginations
10879 Portal Dr., Ste. B
Los Alamitos, CA 90720
(800) 942-6487
www.cigift.com

Archival information: for Bryce & Madeline stickers, acid-free, lignin-free; for Mary Engelbreit stickers, acid-free, lignin-free

Creative Memories
P.O. Box 1839
St. Cloud, MN 56302
(800) 341-5275
www.creativememories.com

Archival information: album is acid-free, lignin-free, and buffered; stickers are acid-free and lignin-free

Cut-It-Up
P.O. Box 287
Gold Run, CA 95717
(916) 646-4646
www.scrapramento.com

Archival information: not applicable

Deja Views, see C-Thru Ruler Company

Delta Technical Coatings
2550 Pellissier Pl.
Whittier, CA 90601
(800) 423-4135
www.deltacrafts.com

Archival information: not applicable

EK Success
P.O. Box 1141
Clifton, NJ 07014
(800) 524-1349
www.eksuccess.com

Archival information: ZIG pens are acid-free, lightfast, fade-proof, waterproof, non-bleeding, pigment ink, smear proof (once dry); conforms to ASTM D-4236, P.A.T. passed for all ZIG Memory System products labeled "Photo Safe"; Stickopotamus stickers are P.A.T. passed

Ellison
25862 Commercentre Dr.
Lake Forest, CA 92630
(800) 253-2238
www.ellison.com

Archival information: not applicable (Ellison does not sell ready-to-use die cuts, only the equipment to make them)

Extra Special Products
P.O. Box 777
Greenville, OH 45331
(937) 548-9388
www.extraspecial.com

Archival information: not applicable

Family Treasures, Inc.
24922 Anza Dr., Unit A
Valencia, CA 91355
(661) 294-1330
www.familytreasures.com

Fiskars, Inc.
7811 W. Stewart Ave.
Wausau, WI 54401
(715) 842-2091
www.fiskars.com

Archival information: not applicable

Frances Meyer, Inc.
P.O. Box 3088
Savannah, GA 31402
(800) 372-6237
www.francesmeyer.com

Archival information for stickers: acid-free, lignin-free, sticker paper pH 7.8–8.5, sticker adhesive pH 9.4

The Gifted Line
Michel & Company (from the John Grossman Collection of Antique Images)
P.O. Box 3625
Culver City, CA 90231
(800) 533-7263
www.michelcom.com

Archival information for The Gifted Line stickers: acid-free, lignin-free, UV coated

Mary Engelbreit stickers, see Creative Imaginations

Mrs. Grossman's Paper Company
P.O. Box 4467
Petaluma, CA 94955
(800) 429-4549
www.mrsgrossmans.com

Archival information for stickers: Each of Mrs. Grossman's sticker modules (one perforated section of a strip) is coded on the back with an abbreviation indicating the size and type of sticker. (For example, DGRF stands for double giant reflection.) The various types of stickers have different pH levels, as follows. All are P.A.T. passed and lignin-free. R, DR, DDR, G, DG, E, DL: pH 7.0–8.6; O, DO: pH 7.0; RF, DRF, GRF, DGRF: pH 7.8; S, DS, DDS: pH 7.0–7.5; PW, DPW, GPW, DLPW: pH 7.2.

The Paper Patch
P.O. Box 414
Riverton, UT 84065
(800) 397-2737
website unknown

Archival information: acid-free, lignin-free, buffered, all papers P.A.T. passed, pH 7.0–8.5, all papers passed ANSI/NISO standards for permanence

Pebbles in My Pocket
368 S. Industrial Dr.
Orem, UT 84058
(800) 438-8153
www.pebblesinmypocket.com

Archival information: die cuts and laser-cut corners are acid-free, lignin-free, and buffered; sticker letters are acid-free